Big Fat Cat
AND
THE MAGIC PIE SHOP

Takahiko Mukoyama
Tetsuo Takashima
with studio ET CETERA

월북

• 영어를 이해하는 데 굳이 번역문은 필요하지 않다는 저자의 뜻에 따라 우리말 해석을 싣지 않았습니다. 하지만
이 책을 다 본 후에 정확한 번역을 확인하고 싶다면 윌북 영어 카페에 들러주세요. 언제든 환영합니다.
cafe.naver.com/everville

PREVIOUSLY IN THE BIG FAT CAT SERIES
지금까지의 **BIG FAT CAT** 시리즈

‘파이 헤븐’ — 파이의 천국. 마침내 갖게 된 자신의 가게에 한 청년이 붙인 이름입니다. 그러나 현실의 파이 헤븐은 천국과는 동떨어진 곳이에요.

그 청년의 이름은 에드 위시본. 그의 꿈은 파이를 굽는 것. 꿈을 이루기 위해 인구 8천 명이 채 안 되는 작은 마을 에버빌로 옵니다. 가까스로 가게를 개업하고 모든 것이 순조롭게 풀리는 듯하지만, 웬일인지 손님이 오지 않아 날마다 파리만 날리기 일쑤이지요. 단골손님이라고 해봐야 블루베리 파이만 먹어 치우는 뚱보 도둑고양이가 고작이니까요. 앞날은 어둡지만 타고난 낙천가인 에드는 어떻게든 되리라 믿으며 가볍게 생각합니다.

그러던 어느 날 마을의 재개발 계획으로 인해 에드의 가게는 불도저에 짓밟히고 말아요. 에드는 하루아침에 집도 일터도 잃고, 달랑 가방 하나만 가지고 언제부터인가 데리고 살게 된 고양이를 품에 안은 채 거리로 쫓겨납니다. (〈빅팻캣과 머스터드 파이〉)

Ed Wishbone

Big and Fat
The Cat

해 저무는 거리를 망연자실 걸어가는 에드와 고양이. 그런 에드의 시선을 붙잡은 것은 뉴 에버빌 몰에서 새로운 가게들을 모집한다는 옥외광고. 달리 기댈 곳이 없던 에드는 되든 안 되든 뉴 몰의 오너를 찾아가 면접을 보기로 합니다. 그러나 그곳에는 이미 다른 지원자가 와 있어요. 이름은 제레미 라이트푸트로 에드와 나이도 비슷하고 마찬가지로 파이 가게를 경영하고 있었죠. 그러나 두 사람 사이에는 큰 격차가 있습니다. 제레미는 대부호의 아들인 데다가 대형 파이 체인점인 '좀비 파이'로 성공을 거두고 있었으니까요. 승산 없는 게임이라고 여긴 에드가 그 자리에서 도망치듯 빠져나오려는데, 에드의 올곧은 성품이 마음에 든 뉴 몰의 오너가 선뜻 기회를 주는 거예요. "오늘 문 닫을 시간까지 한 달 치 가게세를 지불하기만 하면 가게 하나를 자네에게 주겠네."

믿기지 않는 행운에 반신반의하며 에드는 은행으로 달려갑니다. 가진 돈을 몽땅 털어 뉴 몰로 되돌아오는 에드. 그러나 뉴 몰에 들어서기 직전 블랙 리무진이 돌진해서 에드를 치고 돈가방을 가로채더니 어둠 저편으로 사라지고 마네요. 심지어 고양이마저 자취를 감춥니다. (《빅팻캣, 도시로 가다》)

Billy Bob

The Owner of the New Everville Mall

Jeremy Lightfoot Jr.

의식을 반쯤 잃은 채 거리를 방황하는 에드. 추위와 피로로 정신을 잃었다가 깨어보니 낯선 거리의 모퉁입니다. 에드를 도와준 사람은 월리라 불리는 노인으로 노숙자 같아요. 월리는 폐허를 방불케 하는 이 거리가 일명 '고스트 애비뉴'라며, 에드를 허물어져가는 영화관 안의 거처로 데려갑니다. 그곳에서 에드는 사람들에게서 잊혀진, 그야 말로 '고스트'나 다름없는 생활을 하고 있는 노숙자들과 만나요. 그리고 지금까지 미처 몰랐던 어두운 세상의 단면을 목격합니다.

가게는 물론 전 재산을 잃고 상심한 에드에게 월리는 '자네는 파이를 굽는다고는 하지만 참된 파이맛을 내는 법은 모르는 듯해'라고 충고해요. 일찍이 에드의 어머니는 파이 굽기에 관해서는 누구나 인정하는 명인이었습니다. 돌아가신 어머니가 해주신 말씀과도 일맥상통하는 월리의 말을 듣고 에드는 눈물을 흘리며 긴 밤을 지새워요.

"파이는 달콤할 때도 시큼할 때도 있지만, 사랑하는 사람과 먹으면 언제나 달콤한 법이란다."

Professor Willy

아침이 밝아오자 에드는 버려진 드럼통과 여기저기서 끌어 모은 재료를 이용해서 윌리 일행을 위한 파이를 만듭니다. 모양새가 화려하지는 않아도 정성이 담긴 소박한 파이. 에드가 처음으로 자부심을 느끼며 만든, 에드만이 만들 수 있는 파이예요. 그 파이를 한 입 베어물고 행복한 듯 미소를 짓는 윌리 일행을 보고 에드는 지금까지 자신에게 무엇이 부족했는지 깨닫습니다.

행방불명이던 고양이도 무사히 돌아오자, 이제 새로운 한 걸음을 내딛으려는 에드. 그러나 마을의 재개발 계획이 고스트 애비뉴에도 들이닥쳐 또다시 거부할 수 없는 운명의 소용돌이에 휩싸이게 될 줄은 미처 몰랐습니다……. (〈빅팻캣과 고스트 애비뉴〉)

The "Ghosts"

You know this town...

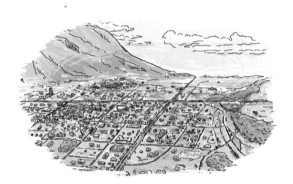

You know this street...

And you know this man.

But some things have changed since the last time you saw
him.

It has been a long month for Ed Wishbone.

"George! Cherry! We need more cherry!" Ed shouted as he handed the last slice of cherry pie to a customer.

George was pulling a freshly baked banana chocolate pie out of the barrel^{드럼통} oven. He shouted to Ed.

"Gotcha!"^{got you}

George handed the pie over to Paddy and started running down the street to the old cinema. They kept several extra^{여분의} pies there, just in case.

"W-where do you want this?" Paddy asked Ed.

    "Below the counter somewhere," Ed told Paddy ^{서둘러} hurriedly as he turned back to a waiting customer.

    "I'm sorry, ma'am. What can I get for you today?"

    "I'll take a slice of that new lemon pie... and of course, two slices of blueberry, as ^{평소의} usual."

    "That'll be 75 cents."

    "Are you sure? I feel like I'm ^{속이다} cheating you. Paying you only 75 cents for such a wonderful pie."

    "Thank you. But don't worry. We're doing fine."

    "Well, God ^{축복하다} bless you. I hope you can do something about this long waiting line ^{그래도} though."

    "I'm sorry, ma'am. I'll try. Have a nice day."

    "You too, now."

Ed ducked down under the counter for a moment and
whispered to Paddy.

_{머리를 홱 숙이다}

"I'm going to check the pies in the oven. Watch the shop for
me, okay, Pad?"

"Uh... I-I'm not sure, Ed."

Paddy looked doubtful but Ed was already dashing out the
side door.

_{망설이는}

Behind the trailer, there was a small outdoor kitchen. Ed and
George had made three ovens out of barrels, steel panels, and
pieces of wire. The smell of butter and sugar was everywhere.

Willy and the cat were playing around while Frank watched
nearby, sitting in an old toy wagon. At least, Willy was playing.
The cat's eyes were much more serious, focused on the pies in the
oven.

_{진지한}

Ed spoke to Willy as he opened the first oven and peeked ^(얼른 보다) inside.

"Will, please keep that cat out of the kitchen. It's not clean."

"Oh, c'mon Ed. He deserves a piece, too," Willy protested. ^(~할 가치가 있다) ^(이의를 달다)

"That cat already ate two whole pies this morning!"

Ed pointed his finger at the cat. The cat paid no attention. ^(기울이다) ^(주의)

BeeJees grunted. He was sitting nearby on an old tractor tire. ^(투덜거리다)

"That cat bit me when I tried to pet him." ^(어루만지다)

"Bit you?!" George said.

He had returned from the theater with a cherry pie in his hands. He was still out of breath. He showed his free hand to BeeJees. There were four great big slashes on his forearm. ^(베인 상처)

"Look at this, man. That cat *attacked* me when I was baking a blueberry pie! I was almost killed, man!"

"George, watch out!"

Ed shouted just in time for George to dodge the cat's jump [피하다]
from behind. The cat soared [치솟다] through the air, a few inches below
the cherry pie in George's hand. The cat landed and turned back
in a very angry [화난] motion. George looked at the cat and gulped [침을 꿀꺽 삼키다].

"Oh-oh... He's gonna [going to] kill me now."

"George, RUN!" everybody yelled [소리 지르다] together.

George was already running, the cat right behind him in full
speed. The two dashed through the kitchen and went running
down Ghost Avenue as everybody laughed behind. Ed laughed
too, holding a fresh-baked country cheesecake in his hand.

It had been a long month. A long month on Ghost Avenue.

It had all begun as a simple joke. George, who used to be a
handyman, had made Ed a sign that said "Ed's Magic Pie Shop."
The sign was a token of appreciation for the pies that Ed baked
for the people in the cinema. Ed had hung it happily in front of
the cinema without much thought.

But the other homeless residents of Ghost Avenue who had
heard stories about free pie, saw the sign and came in to get some
for themselves. Some of them even left a few dimes and nickels.

George soon found an old deserted trailer at the northern
end of Ghost Avenue and had painted it with leftover paint. The
trailer was just the right size to create a small kitchen space, so Ed
moved his outdoor kitchen there.

As the days went by, more and more people started to come
buy pies, and not all of them were homeless. A few curious
passing cars started to stop by, and several kind women who lived
nearby had come to buy a slice of pie in the spirit of charity. They
returned for more when they found out the pies were actually
good.

Now the cat was coming back down the street. The cat's
whiskers were covered with something red. It pretty much
suggested the fate of the cherry pie. George came around the
corner after the cat, covered with the rest of the cherry pie. Ed
smiled in spite of losing another pie. The others laughed in an
uproar. They laughed so hard that Ed didn't realize Paddy was
shouting.

"E-Ed!!"

Ed finally heard Paddy calling him on the third shout and
waved a hand at him.

"Sorry, Pad. Be back in a minute!"

"N-No, Ed!! You need to come back, n-now!"

Ed's smile faded when he saw that the crowd in front of the
shop had grown. Grown a lot. He stood there in awe, his heart
beating faster and faster. He knew something had gone wrong.

Jeremy Lightfoot Jr. was afraid of his father.

He had always been afraid of him, even as a small child.
He felt that his father was always ^{실망하다}disappointed with him, and
^{그래서}therefore, always angry.

He never knew his mother. There was nobody to protect him
from his father when he was a child. So he tried ^{온 힘을 다해}desperately to
be a good son. He tried and tried, but ^{그럼에도 불구하고}nevertheless his father was
always angry.

Now, as he stood at the door to his father's ^{서재}study, his hands
were shaking. Jeremy would be thirty-one years old this year, but
he still felt like a ten-year-old boy.

Jeremy's cat, Mr. Jones, appeared out of nowhere and brushed his tail on Jeremy's foot. Jeremy petted Mr. Jones with a slightly
별별 떨다
trembling hand. It made him feel a little better.

"You wait for me here, okay?"

Mr. Jones purred. Jeremy straightened his ^깃collar and tie and took a deep breath. He grabbed the doorknob and after one last
망설임
moment of hesitation, turned it.

"Sir. You asked me to..." Jeremy said in a shaking voice as he stepped inside.

"Shut the door, you ^바보moron."

His father's cold voice filled the room.

22

Jeremy closed the door and stood nervously beside it. His

안절부절못하며

father was watching the morning news on television and didn't
even look back. The new bodyguard, Billy Bob, was standing at
the far wall.

Jeremy didn't know why his father had hired Billy Bob. He

고용하다

already had two-dozen bodyguards around the house. But his
father had told him Billy Bob was different.

And he was. Jeremy had felt it since the first time he had seen
the man. There was a true coldness in the way Billy Bob moved.
And he almost never talked.

"How is your business?" Jeremy's father asked suddenly.
Jeremy was surprised. His father almost never asked him
anything. Feeling a sense of relief,^(안도) Jeremy took a step forward.

"Great, sir. Zombie Pies is really taking off. You should see
the numbers. We're the fastest growing chain in the whole..."

"Good. Close it down."

Jeremy stopped on his first step, stunned in shock.^(아연실색하다)

"Uh... excuse me?"

"I said, close down the pie shops. I need the space to promote^(진척시키다)
the rehabilitation^(재건) project."

Jeremy just stood there, forgetting even to breathe.

"Did you, or did you not, hear me?" his father demanded,^(묻다) still
not moving his eyes from the television screen.

"I... I can't do that, sir. Even if it's your order.^(명령) It's my shop."
Jeremy's voice grew smaller and smaller. "The kids love my
shops. They really love Zombie Pies."

Jeremy's father said nothing. He was watching the television screen in silence. The morning news was showing the top news — something about a government scandal in Washington.

"Please let me keep the shops. I really need this."

"Your so-called shops will last for maybe another six months," Jeremy Lightfoot Sr. said finally. He spoke in a harsh, cold tone.

"Then they'll get tired of your pies and your shops will be forgotten."

"I'll try harder! I'll make it work! Please give me a chance to..."

"Quiet."

"Father..." Jeremy protested.

"I said, shut up!" Jeremy's father suddenly raised his voice. He leaned forward for a closer look at the television screen. "Billy Bob, turn up the sound."

Billy Bob took out the remote control and pushed the volume switch. The voice of a reporter boomed out of the speaker, filling the quiet room with a sudden burst of excitement.

"...As you can see, a small miracle has happened here on the deserted northwest side of Everville. People are returning to this once well-known shopping district. A twenty-nine-year-old man, Ed Wishbone, has started a small pie shop in the ruins of an old trailer. This is his kitchen. He says that all of his utensils are fully sanitized and everything is safe and clean. Let's ask Mr. Wishbone himself about his pies."

The camera moved through the side door of the pie shop and captured a shot of Ed, all red with embarrassment to the rims of his ears. Though his father didn't notice, Jeremy opened his eyes wide when he saw Ed on the screen.

"Do you really make these pies in that backyard? They're really good. Sweet... but not too sweet."

"Uh... thank you."

"Are you thinking of entering the state pie festival this weekend?"

"Pie festival?"

"The Annual State Pie Festival is held this year at the Everville Mall. You should consider entering. The prize this year is twenty thousand dollars!"

"I... I don't know. I really..."

Ed was cut off by the loud applause of the customers outside.

"I think your customers know."

The reporter smiled and gave Ed a wink.

"So now you've seen it, one man's journey to save the old streets of Everville. And from the way people are gathering, who knows? He just might succeed. This is Glen Hamperton reporting from Ever..."

Billy Bob turned the television off. Jeremy Senior had raised his hand in the air.

"This is bad," Jeremy's father said to Billy Bob. "We can't
afford having this man become any more popular than he is
now."

"Yes, sir," Billy Bob replied.

"As for this pie festival..." Jeremy Senior turned his armchair
once more towards his son, took a deep breath, and spoke. "You
might as well have that chance of yours. Stop this man from
winning the contest and perhaps I will reconsider the termination
of your enterprise."

"Will... will you really..."

"Do you, or do you not, want a chance?"

"Yes, sir. I'll try my best."

"Your best is far from enough. Try harder."

That said, Jeremy Senior simply turned away towards Billy
Bob. "Billy Bob, come here."

With that, his father seemed to have forgotten he was there. He could probably stand there for an hour, but his father would never notice him. Jeremy Jr. stepped silently out of the room. Only Mr. Jones was waiting for him there, sitting quietly in the middle of the long, empty hallway. Mr. Jones purred.

"It's okay," Jeremy said in a sad voice. "I'm used to it. Nothing new."

Jeremy picked the cat up and held it close. Its warmth was comforting in the lifeless coldness of his father's house. The floor of the corridor was covered with the most expensive carpet on the market and the ceiling was decorated with golden ornaments.

Jeremy had lived in this huge mansion for his entire life, but had always felt lost in the seemingly endless corridors of the place. It looked so much like his life.

Fabulous, but empty.

"Now, *that* is something you don't see everyday," Ed said to George.

He was staring with widened eyes out of the side door of the Magic Pie Shop. George poked his head out from behind Ed and saw it too.

"Damned if I'm seeing that," George muttered, nearly dropping the apple he was peeling.

The cat was eating a piece of piecrust directly from Frank's hand. If Ed, George, or anybody else tried that, the result would be one less hand.

"Frank's good with animals, that's for sure," George said, shaking his head with disbelief.

"That's not an animal. That's a beast," Ed said, staring at the cat. It glared back at him.

The sunset signaled the end of another day for the Magic Pie Shop. Newly baked pies were lined on the table, ready for tomorrow. They gave off the sweet, spicy smell of hot cinnamon.

Hordes of people who had seen the news came rushing in for pies immediately after the broadcast. Ed sold every single slice of pie in the shop before closing for the day.

"Yo, Ed. Apples done, man. What next?"

George tossed the last peeled apple into the water bucket and washed his hands.

"Wow. You're getting faster everyday. Well... maybe you can help Willy and Pad clean the ovens."

"Sure thing," George said and went out the back door.

The sun was almost down. Orange rays came through the doorway. Ed whistled a tune as he knelt down below the counter to get a new bowl.

"Wishbone."

Ed froze as he got up. He found himself face to face with Jeremy Lightfoot Jr. He also noticed the big shadow standing behind him.

"I'm afraid we're closed," Ed replied, almost a whisper.

George and the others were in the backyard kitchen. He was alone in the shop. Jeremy tossed a flier on top of the counter.

"Take it. It's the entry form for this weekend's pie contest."

Ed remained motionless.

"Take it, Wishbone!" Jeremy said abruptly. This made Ed grab the flier. "You think you're so good. Come prove it."

"I don't want to be in a contest," Ed protested to Jeremy. "This shop is all I want. Please leave us alone."

Jeremy made a face of 혐오 disgust.

"You 거짓말하다 lying 겁쟁이 coward," he said. "You would love to win, but you're afraid you'll lose. I bet you've never 장담하다 ... 싸우다 fought for anything in your whole life."

Ed kept his eyes on Billy Bob. But Jeremy's words echoed in his ear.

"Wishbone! Stop 무시하다 ignoring me!"

Jeremy's voice rose even higher in anger. He didn't know why he was getting so 화난 mad at this man he hardly knew. He didn't even know why he had come here.

"Shop! You call this 쓰레기 dump a shop!? A Magic Pie Shop, huh? What does *magic* mean anyway!? Do you disappear or something?"

Jeremy 낚아채다 snatched the sign of the Magic Pie Shop. He threw it on the ground and stepped on it.

"You need to..."

Jeremy never finished his sentence. Ed had suddenly grabbed him by the shoulder. Jeremy was caught by surprise. The man in front of him had suddenly become angry. Jeremy noticed this but couldn't understand why. He kept his foot on the sign.

"What are you..."

"Take your foot off my shop!" Ed said in a surprisingly strong voice.

"It's just a sign..."

Jeremy was cut off again.

"I said, take it off!"

Ed shoved Jeremy off the sign. ^{때밀다} Jeremy lost balance and fell down on his back.

Billy Bob's large hands grabbed Ed, pulled him over the counter and threw him to the ground. Ed scrambled over to the ^{기어가다} sign on the ground and covered it with the only thing he had. His body.

Billy Bob was instantly above him, kicking him on the side of his chest. It hurt badly and Ed couldn't stop coughing. Dust was ^{가슴} ^{기침하다} ^{먼지} flying all around him.

"Hey... you don't need to..."

Jeremy said to Billy Bob, but couldn't finish. He had seen the cold, hard look on Billy Bob's face. Billy Bob kicked Ed a second time. Ed coughed in pain again, but refused to get up. He gritted ^{거부하다} ^{(이를) 악물다} his teeth together to stop coughing and looked straight up at Jeremy. He tasted blood in his mouth, but was no longer scared.

34

"You're just like me," Ed said.

Billy Bob kicked him again.

"What?" Jeremy cried out. "Are you out of your mind!? I'm exactly not like you! I'm rich, I'm smart, I'm... rich, I'm..."

"You don't know what a pie is made of."

Jeremy tried hard to laugh but did not succeed. He shouted desperately at Billy Bob.

"This man is out of his mind. You kicked him too much!"

Ed sailed. This angered Jeremy even more. He cried out.

"What do you know!? What the ^(강조) fuck do you know!?"

Billy Bob raised his foot over Ed's head. Ed ^{최다} squeezed his eyes shut. But before Billy Bob could bring his foot down, a flash of red flew through the air. Billy Bob took a step back. Jeremy let out a cry of surprise at the same time.

"What..."

Ed opened his eyes and looked up.

Pies were flying through the air!

Jeremy frantically wiped hot pie from his face, but as he was
doing this, some got in his mouth. He stopped in silence. Several
pies hit him but he didn't seem to notice. He just looked straight
at Ed.

Billy Bob had mopped the pie off of his chest and was coming
back at Ed. But this time, Jeremy shot his hand out in front of
Billy Bob and stopped him.

"That's enough," Jeremy said to Billy Bob.

Jeremy and Ed looked at each other one last time. The pies
had also stopped (probably out of ammunition).

"See you at the contest," Jeremy said.

Jeremy straightened his tie and walked off
silently. Billy Bob, after a moment of
hesitation, followed.

When Jeremy and Billy Bob were clearly out of sight, George
slid down from the roof and ran over to Ed.

"Ed! Man! You all right?"

Ed stood up. In his hands, he held the sign George had
painted for him. It was broken in half.

"George... I'm sorry."

"Hey, man, it's just a sign. I'll paint you another one
tomorrow."

George laughed as if nothing had happened. It was such a
light-hearted laugh that Ed smiled a little too.

"Magic ain't in the sign, man. Cheer up! We won!"

With that, Paddy and Willy let out a great big cheer of victory
from the roof of the trailer. George patted Ed on the back. Ed
gradually began to laugh out loud too.

Everyone was laughing except for the cat. It just happened to
come around the shop at that moment and was confronting the
most shocking scene of its life.

38

Midnight.

A few hours later, the "ghosts" of Ghost Avenue were safely gathered around the fire inside the cinema. Ed had pretty much recovered and was now mixing ingredients for his new pie.

회복하다   (요리) 재료

Everybody watched with curiosity as Ed took out a jar of pickles. A look of doubt crossed their faces as Ed minced the pickles and threw them into the bowl. But they managed to remain quiet while Ed added ingredients such as boiled eggs, grated cheese, and spinach. When Ed reached for the small yellow bottle, however, Willy finally spoke out.

의심   교차하다   다지다   (remain) 할 수 있다   갈린   시금치

"Ed! That's mustard," Willy cried as Ed poured mustard from the bottle into the bowl. Ed heard, but continued to pour the yellow liquid until he had mixed the last drop into the recipe. Everybody watched with sour faces. Ed looked around the table, saw the faces, and said with a smile, "It's okay. It's my new pie."

액체

"Ed. That's mustard," Willy repeated simply.

"Of course, it's mustard. It's a mustard pie."

This caused everybody to grimace. _{얼굴을 찡그리다}

"It's not that bad," Ed quickly added.

Everyone replied with groans and deep sighs. Ed, a little _{불평의 소리} frustrated, took a freshly baked pie from under the table and placed it in front of everybody. _{불만스러운}

"Here. I baked one earlier today. Have a taste."

Everyone took a step back from the table. A faint smell of mustard was mixed with the crisp smell of piecrust. _{파삭파삭한}

"Go ahead. Have a taste," Ed insisted. _{주장하다}

The men looked at each other hopefully, but no one volunteered. _{자원하다} Reluctantly, they played a game of scissors-paper-stone to decide. _{마지못해서} _{가위바위보} Willy lost. Willy turned towards the pie with a sad look and found Ed twitching his eyebrows at him. He smiled quickly. _{씰룩거리다} _{눈썹}

"Uh, Ed. I'm happy to have the honor of participating in _{명예} _{참가하다} this... this science experiment." _{과학} _{실험}

"It's not an experiment," Ed said.

"Oh, I'm sure that my sacrifice will someday be useful to the further development of mankind. Well, so long everybody."

Willy waved his hand and picked up a piece of the mustard pie. He raised it to his nose and smelled it. Everyone held their breath. After a moment, Willy collapsed to the floor. The others burst out laughing.

"The smell!? Just with the smell!? No way!!" Ed shouted.

By this time, George, Paddy and Frank were all laughing so hard that they could hardly keep standing.

"I'm telling you! It's not that bad!"

Ed was angry and the others were busy laughing. No one except BeeJees realized that Willy had fallen down awkwardly. BeeJees leaned over the table to whisper to Willy, who was still lying on the floor.

"Hey, Willy. You can get up now. We got your point. Willy?"

BeeJees's face turned white when he saw that Willy was lying face down.

"No! It's not the pie! It's his heart! It's doing it again!"

BeeJees jumped across the table to Willy. The others were still laughing.

"What?" Ed asked.

He could not hear what BeeJees had said because of the laughter. But everyone stopped laughing when BeeJees held up Willy's limp body.
축 늘어진

"Prof! C'mon! Prof!"

Ed froze. He couldn't understand what was happening. He cried out in almost sheer panic.
완전한

"BeeJees! What the hell is going on!?"
(강조)

"Don't worry. It's not your pie," BeeJees turned back and replied quickly. Sweat was running down his forehead. "Willy's heart is in a real bad condition."
땀

All Ed could say was, "Why isn't he in a hospital?"

"Because hospitals cost money."
비용이 들다

"Use mine."

Ed took his wallet out instantly and held it out to BeeJees. A cold feeling was rising up in his heart. Willy wasn't moving. His mouth was half open, as if he had stopped breathing.
지갑

Grasping the situation at last, George and Paddy rushed over to Willy and started slapping his face. The night suddenly seemed a lot darker and colder.
파악하다   상황   찰싹 때리다

42

"Hospital costs lots of money. At least two grand a week. And that's without any treatment," BeeJees said to Ed as he was giving CPR to Willy.

"He's not responding!" Paddy cried out, almost in tears.

"Oh no... This is bad, man. This is really bad."

George was sweating hard too. This was the first time Ed had seen George with a serious face. But Ed still couldn't move. All he could do was stand there and ask in a dumbfounded voice, "Isn't there a phone somewhere? We need an ambulance."

"You know there isn't a single working phone on this street," BeeJees said to Ed. He was angry. Probably not angry at Ed, but angry.

Beejees took a deep breath, trying to calm down.

"Besides..., no ambulance would come here at this time of night."

"Then what are we supposed to do? He's dying, isn't he?"

"Pray," BeeJees answered.

BeeJees, George, and Paddy were trying to do everything they could. But anybody could see this wasn't enough. Ed looked desperately around the theater and found a rusty shopping cart by the wall. He grabbed the cart and a few old blankets and hurried over to Willy.

"We have to get him to a hospital."

Ed reached for Willy's hand but BeeJees slapped his arm away.

"Don't!"

"Why not!? For heaven's sake!"

"He wanted to die, Wishbone. If he's going to die, let him die here."

"That's insane!"

"Wishbone. You're just making this harder. Let him go."

Ed reached for Willy again. BeeJees started to stop him, but this time, Ed pushed him away and said to George, "C'mon and help me. We have to get him to a hospital."

George nodded and started helping Ed wrap Willy in one of the blankets. Together, they carried Willy over to the shopping cart. BeeJees just sat there on the ground shaking his head.

"I'm telling you, Wishbone. You're just increasing everyone's pain."

Ed finished tucking Willy into the blanket and turned back
to BeeJees. He was scared. Part of him knew that BeeJees was
probably right. But another part of him, the warmer, stronger
part of him spoke.

"I know I'm naive. I just don't want to give up. I've given up
too many things already."

The shopping cart flew through the theater doors, Ed and
George pushing it from behind.

BeeJees watched the doors swing from the force of the passing
shopping cart. He knew what was going to happen. He slumped
to the ground, biting his lower lip as the tears came, one by one,
down his dry cheek.

"Damn it, Wishbone. Why can't you understand? It's too
late. We're all too late."

The night outside was cold and quiet. The moon was almost full, with a perfect sky behind it — no clouds at all. There was no one in sight. A car passed every once in a while, but other than that, everything was silent except for the rattle of their shopping cart.

Ed and George pushed the cart down Ghost Avenue until they came to the intersection of Lake Every Drive. They crossed the intersection carefully and continued walking south. The hospital was about a mile further down the road. It had been easy until then. But when they entered the downtown district, the road changed uphill.

It was not a steep incline. Perhaps you wouldn't notice it if you were walking. But it made a pretty big difference if you were a child or a jogger — or even two men pushing a shopping cart.

The rattle of the rusted cart suddenly broke off when one of the front wheels snapped free. The cart was forced to a stop. Ed knelt down and examined the broken wheel.

George came over to Ed and whispered to him, "No way we can repair this."

George was right. A sense of unease filled Ed as he said, "I guess we'll have to carry the cart."

"Maybe I can carry Willy on my back," George suggested.

"It... might not be a good idea to rock him too much. Besides we still have a mile to go. Can you take the front end? I'll get the back."

"No problem."

George nodded.

And so they went. Two shadows in the moonlight carrying a man in a shopping cart. Sweat rolled down Ed's face, although the first hundred steps were not hard.

But after ten minutes, the weight of the cart started to feel like the weight of a small car. Ed's arms and feet were getting weaker and weaker by the moment.

Ed glanced back over his shoulder. He shouldn't have. Fear ran through him as he realized that they still had more than half way to go. The hospital was a small red glow at the top of the hill. It wasn't that far, but it seemed miles away.

The only thing that kept Ed moving was Willy's lifeless face lying within the pile of musty^(곰팡이 핀) blankets.

He had to keep walking. He had to.

Son. You are a baker.

Professor Willy was the first person who had ever called him a baker. He would never forget that. He would never, ever forget that.

One at a time, he took careful steps forward. His legs were weak now. One wrong step and he might lose balance.

As they passed the elementary school, Ed thought he heard someone say something in a really soft voice. He thought that maybe George was saying something to encourage^(용기를 돋우다) himself. But it wasn't George. He could see that, even from behind.

Then who —

"Willy?" Ed said.

George stopped and looked back. Willy's mouth was moving slightly. Ed leaned forward and listened carefully. At first, he thought Willy was just breathing. But then he was able to hear the soft sounds coming from Willy's mouth.

"He's... singing," Ed said to George with an amazed[놀란] look.

"Singing?" George gasped[헐떡거리다] and listened. "Oh, yeah. I hear it too."

It was such a soft and tender[부드러운] voice.

Ed and George started to walk again, but somehow[웬일인지] it was easier this time. The hospital seemed closer and the cart seemed lighter. Ed noticed the full moon in the sky for the first time. And in spite of all the chaos[혼돈], it was still beautiful.

A comfortable breeze[바람] circled around them. George began to sing along with Willy. It was a song Ed had heard millions of times, but he had never realized how beautiful it was until now.

Tears formed in his eyes. There were so many things he still had to learn. The world was so huge and so full of surprises.

The world is not a mustard pie, Ed.

No, it wasn't.

Ed closed his eyes and listened to Willy and George singing. And after a moment, he too, joined the song.

I see trees of green, red roses too

꽃이 피다
I see them bloom for me and you

And I think to myself

What a wonderful world

I see skies of blue, clouds of white

축복받은　　　　　　신성한
The bright blessed day and the dark sacred night

And I think to myself

What a wonderful world

I hear babies cry, I watch them grow

They'll learn much more than I'll ever know

And I think to myself

What a wonderful world

Yes I think to myself

What a wonderful world

Door.

Emergency.
_{응급}

Get help.

These were the only thoughts left in Ed's head when they finally reached the emergency entrance of the Everville Hospital. He somehow found some final dregs of strength in his legs and wobbled up to the doors.
_{찌꺼기} _힘
_{비틀거리다}

They were locked. Ed banged his fist on the doors.
_{세게 치다} _{주먹}

"Someone! Someone, help us! We need help!"

The lights were dark inside. Nobody answered Ed's call.

Ed took a quick look at the shopping cart. Willy had stopped singing and was as quiet as before. George was totally exhausted and was down on his hands and knees. Ed wanted to give up and lie down too, but he continued to hit the door.
_{지친}

Then suddenly, the sound of a window opening came from above.

Ed backed away a few steps and found a nurse looking down
at them suspiciously.
미심쩍은 듯이

"Ma'am, we need help," Ed said.

The nurse didn't answer, but her eyes studied Ed and the
others carefully — their dirty, ripped clothing, Willy's long beard,
찢어진
and the rusted old shopping cart.

"Please. We need a doctor. If it's money, I have some. And I
promise I'll get more in a few days."

The nurse started to close the windows.

"No! Please! We really need help! Here!" Ed shouted
desperately as he emptied his wallet on the sidewalk. He scattered
비우다   흩뿌리다
small change and a few dollar bills around him. "This is all the
잔돈
money I have now, but...!!"

The window closed shut with a cold sound. Ed was left in the
dark with only silence for an answer.

"Please... we..."

Ed's voice faded as he slumped down on the ground.

George crawled over to Ed and put his hands on Ed's shoulders. Looking at George's face, Ed realized that George had known this would happen. But he had helped him anyway.

"At least we tried, man."

George smiled. It was a true smile.

"I bet the Prof's happy too. Yo, man. Maybe it's time to give up. Leave things to good old Jesus upstairs."

Ed sat still on the concrete. He knew George was right. Just as BeeJees had been right all along.

Ed gripped his thighs and lowered his head close to the ground. He felt hope running out of him. He knew he was about to give up.

Ed had almost never prayed in his life, but at that moment, he prayed from the bottom of his heart. He prayed for courage. The courage not to give up.

"Yo, c'mon Ed," George called.

As Ed was getting up, something fell out of his chest pocket.
떠다니다
It floated in the air for a moment, then landed silently on the
ground. Ed picked it up.

"Yo. Let's go home. I think Willy's just sleeping. He'll be fine
until tomorrow morning."

George caught Ed under the arm and helped him to his feet.
Ed was still holding the flier. His eyes were glued to the words
(풀로) 붙이다
printed on it.

As he read those words, something Willy had said to him a
while before circled around his mind.

Ed. Willy had said. *You are a baker.*

You are a baker.

You are a baker.

TO BE CONTINUED

Big Fat Cat

AND

THE MAGIC SHOP

PIE

꼼꼼히 읽어보기

대화문에 대해서, 잠깐

〈빅팻캣과 매직 파이 숍〉 어떠셨어요?

이번 작품은 대화가 많이 나오는 바람에 이해하기 까다로운 표현들이 많아서 애를 먹은 친구들도 있었을지 모르겠네요. 3권 〈빅팻캣과 고스트 애비뉴〉에서는 '건너뛰고 읽는 기술'에 초점을 맞추어 설명했습니다. 이번 작품에서도 어려운 부분이 있다면 '건너뛰기' 기술을 종종 활용하시기를 바랍니다. 재미가 없다면 독서라 할 수 없습니다. 도중에 막혀서 짜증을 내기보다는 마음 편히 건너뛰고 읽으면 오히려 이야기를 즐길 수 있습니다.

그러나 대화문은 작품에서 핵심을 차지합니다. 대화문까지 건너뛰면 내용 파악이 잘 안 되어서 불안해질 수도 있지요. 이렇듯 대화문은 중요합니다. 하지만 사실 일반 영어 문장에 비해 더 어렵죠. 알듯 말듯 애매한 느낌이 들어서 마음이 편치 않은 분들도 있으리라고 생각합니다.

이처럼 대화문이 어려운 데는 분명한 원인이 있습니다 그 원인만 파악하면 까다로운 대화문도 두려워할 필요가 없습니다. 대체 대화문은 왜 어려울까요? 우선 그 원인부터 생각해봅시다.

'관용어'는 주문이다

원래 입말은 글말과 달라서 일단 말하고 나면 시간을 두고 고치거나 편집할 수 없습니다. 그리고 글말에 비해 문장의 길이가 짧고 간단하죠. 이런 입말을 글로 옮긴 대화문도 물론 짧고 간단해요. 하지만 영어로 씌어져 있을 때는 결코 쉽지가 않습니다. 영어책을 읽다 보면 이해가 잘 안 가는 대화문이나 의미를 알 수 없는 관용어에 부딪히게 마련이에요. 이런 경우 사전을 찾아봐도 의미가 불분명하거나, 문장이 퍼즐처럼 까다로워서 내용을 파악하기가 힘들죠. 바로 이때 우리는 '정말 어렵다'라고 느끼게 됩니다.

하지만 실제로 영어가 어려운 걸까요? 영어를 구사하는 사람들도 일상 회화를 나눌 때 실제로 이처럼 어렵다고 느끼면서 대화를 나누고 있을까요?

우리말로 대화를 나눌 때를 한번 생각해보세요. 불행이 닥쳤을 때 체념하듯 '다 내 업(業)이다'라고 고풍스런 말투를 쓸 때가 있습니다. 이 '업'이란 단어를 외국인이 들었다고 해보세요. 당연히 '업'이란 단어는 들어본 적이 없으므로 사전에서 찾아 그 뜻을 읽어볼 거예요. 그러면 가장 첫 줄에 나오는 뜻풀이가 '업: 직업의 준말'이라고 나옵니다. 이래서는 사전을 봐도 이해가 되지 않아요. 또한 우리의 정신문화에는 불교관이 비교적 친숙하게 자리 잡고 있지만 문화가 다른 외국인으로서는 감을 잡기 어려울 수밖에 없습니다. 외국인이라면 좀처럼 이해할 수 없는 상황이 되어버리는 것이죠.

물론 실제 일상생활에서 '내 업이다'라고 표현하는 경우는 농담조로 과장해서 말할 때뿐입니다. 일상생활에서 무심코 이런 말투가 튀어나왔다면 다음의 세 가지 이유 중 하나일 거예요.

1. 누군가 말하는 것을 듣고 재미있다고 생각했다.
2. 자신의 성격에 맞는 말투라고 생각했다.
3. 예전부터 비슷한 상황이면 즐겨 쓰던 표현이다.

이 중 어떤 이유라고 해도, 말하고 있는 당사자는 심각한 의미를 느끼고 그 표현을 사용하지는 않습니다. 누군가 말하는 것을 듣고 당시와 비슷한 상황이 벌어지자 자신도 별 의미 없이 사용하는 표현, 바로 이런 표현이 '관용어'예요. 우리말도 그렇지만 영어에도 관용어가 풍부해요.

'관용어'를 사용하는 데 특별한 규칙은 없습니다. 말하자면 관용어란 일종의 '주문'과도 같아서 어떤 표현을 했을 때 그 표현에 대해서 상대가 느끼는 감정이나 반응이 거의 비슷해요. 언제나 같은 효과를 불러일으키므로 기억하고 있으면 편하지만, 관용어의 의미를 모를 경우 이해하지 못하는 것은 당연한 일이죠.

위의 일러스트를 보고 '말풍선에 적당한 문구를 넣어주세요'라고 미국인에게 부탁하면 아마 돌아올 답은 몇 가지로 정해져 있을 거예요. 실제로 위와 비슷한 상황이 연출된다면 당사자가 하는 말도 역시 비슷할 거예요. 이런 장면에서 흔히 사용되는 '관용어'를 실제 회화에서도 사용하기 때문입니다.

회화와 모스 부호의 공통점

관용어는 줄곧 대화를 할 때 매우 간단한 문장들 사이에 들어갑니다. 구성을 살펴보면 모스 부호와 비슷해요. 이를테면 뚜─ 뚜─ 하는 소리처럼 별 의미 없는 문장이 계속되다가 탁 치면서 리듬감을 주듯이 관용어구가 들어가요.

회화는 이런 느낌으로 진행됩니다. 회화를 대화문으로 옮겨보면 다음의 예문과 같이 파란 글자로 표시한 '일반 문장' 사이에 주황색으로 표시한 '관용어구'가 리듬감 있게 삽입되는 것을 알 수 있습니다.

**Hi! How are you? I saw that new horror movie "Big Fat Cat"
Yesterday. It was horrible. Bad as can be. I hope they never
make a sequel. Well, see you later!**

회화는 언어 중에서도 특수한 분야에 속합니다. 공부한다기보다 자주 접해서 익숙해져
야 해요. '아, 이런 상황에서는 이렇게 말하는구나.' '음, 그래도 이렇게 말하는 게 내 말투
같다.' '그렇군. 이 정도의 반응이면 효과적이네.' 이처럼 경험이 반복되어 쌓이다 보면 회
화를 주고받을 수 있게 돼요. 간단한 문장 사이에 살짝 펀치를 가하는 효과를 주는 '관용어
구'를 삽입하면서. 바로 이것이 '수다를 떠는 것'이에요. 또 '관용어구'를 말하는 동안 머릿
속으로는 잠깐 쉬면서 뒤이어 무슨 말을 할지 생각하는 여유도 확보할 수 있습니다.

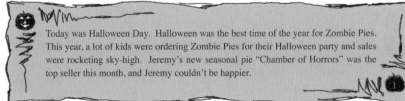

Today was Halloween Day. Halloween was the best time of the year for Zombie Pies.
This year, a lot of kids were ordering Zombie Pies for their Halloween party and sales
were rocketing sky-high. Jeremy's new seasonal pie "Chamber of Horrors" was the
top seller this month, and Jeremy couldn't be happier.

rocketing = 로켓처럼 날아오르다

소설에서 대화문을 읽다가 '어휴, 어려워!'라고 느끼는 표현은 대개 '관용구'입니다. 따라서 처음 읽을 때는 이해가 되지 않더라도 걱정하지 않기를 바랍니다. 이번 작품 〈빅팻캣과 매직 파이 숍〉에는 지금까지의 Big Fat Cat 시리즈보다 일상적이고 다채로운 회화가 많이 나와요. '관용어'와 '슬랭(속어)' 등도 종종 나와요. 그래서 이번 해설에서는 '관용구'에 밑줄을 긋고 자세한 설명을 하고 있는 것이죠.

늘 말해왔지만, '관용구'를 일일이 암기할 필요는 없습니다. 설사 암기했더라도 자신의 성격과 맞지 않으면 평생 입 밖에 낼 일이 없지요. 대신 무심코 읽다가 재미있다고 느낀 표현이 있으면 자연스럽게 머리에 남게 되는 거예요. 그 관용구가 나중에는 실제로 활용할 수 있는 표현입니다. 그러므로 활용하지도 않을 표현까지 암기하기보다는 다시 한번 영어 본문을 읽어보는 쪽이 훨씬 유익해요.

보통 '영어 회화'를 배울 때 기본적으로 이런 '관용어'를 많이 암기하도록 권합니다. 물론 '관용구'를 많이 암기하면 커뮤니케이션이 다소 늘기도 하지만 결국에는 한계에 부딪히게 되지요. 또 이런 방법으로 공부하게 되면 자신의 성격에 어울리지 않는 표현까지 쓰게 될 수도 있어요. 비록 돌아가는 한이 있더라도 자신만의 영어 말투를 찾아서 하나하나 자신에게 맞는 '관용구'를 익히는 편이 진정한 영어를 배울 수 있는 길이랍니다.

'누가 어떤 관용구를 사용하고 있지?' '다른 캐릭터가 이 관용구를 사용하면 어떻게 인상이 바뀔까?' 그리고 지금까지는 미처 살펴보지 못했던 목소리의 크기, 대화문과 대화문 사이의 행간, 대화문의 길이 등도 느끼면서 다시 한번 〈빅팻캣과 매직 파이 숍〉을 읽어보기 바랍니다.

자, 이제 다음 페이지부터 본격적으로 Big Fat Cat 방식의 영어 회화 교실로 들어가볼까요?

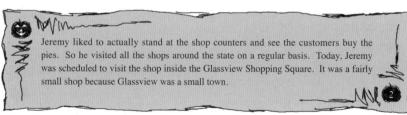

Jeremy liked to actually stand at the shop counters and see the customers buy the pies. So he visited all the shops around the state on a regular basis. Today, Jeremy was scheduled to visit the shop inside the Glassview Shopping Square. It was a fairly small shop because Glassview was a small town.

basis = 주기

pp.14~15 우선 첫 대화문부터

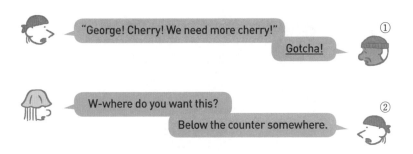

"George! Cherry! We need more cherry!"

Gotcha! ①

W-where do you want this? ②

Below the counter somewhere.

첫 대화문이 나오는 부분은 본문의 14쪽입니다.

이야기의 막이 오르자마자 위세 좋게 지시를 내리고 있는 에드. 지금까지와는 인상이 조금 달라졌네요. 근소한 차이지만 말투도 바뀌었어요. 결코 거친 말투는 아니지만 바쁘기 때문에 최소한의 단어만을 이용하여 말을 하고 있습니다.

②의 대화문을 예로 들어볼까요. 지금까지의 에드라면 정중하게 Please put it below the counter somewhere라고 표현했겠지만, 이 문장에서 에드는 생략할 수 있는 부분은 다 생략해서 말하고 있어요. 이번 작품에서는 에드의 대화문이 전반적으로 짧아지고 있다는 점을 유의하며 읽어보세요.

조지의 대화문 중에 Gotcha! (①)는 Got you!의 줄임 형태예요. 직역하면 '너를 잡는다'이지만 실제 의미는 '알았다!'는 의미입니다. 일반적으로 사용하는 yes나 sure의 의미에서 더 나아가 '나한테 맡겨'라는 자신감과 활력이 담겨 있는 표현이죠. 바로 이런 표현이 '관용어'입니다. 단 Gotcha는 꽤 거친 말투가 입에 밴 사람이 쓰는 표현이므로, 조지와 같은 상황에 처한 경우가 아니라면 좀처럼 사용할 일이 없을지도 몰라요.

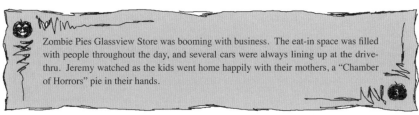

Zombie Pies Glassview Store was booming with business. The eat-in space was filled with people throughout the day, and several cars were always lining up at the drive-thru. Jeremy watched as the kids went home happily with their mothers, a "Chamber of Horrors" pie in their hands.

booming = 경기가 좋아지다

I'm sorry, ma'am. <u>What can I get for you today?</u>

I'll take a slice of that new lemon pie... and <u>of course</u>, two slices of blueberrt, <u>as usual</u>.

<u>That'll be 75 cents.</u>

<u>Are you sure?</u> I feel like I'm cheating you. Paying you only 75 cents for such a wonderful pie.

<u>Thank you.</u> But don't worry. We're doing fine.

①

Well, <u>God bless you.</u> I hope you can do something about this long waiting line though.

②

I'm sorry, ma'am. I'll try. <u>Have a nice day.</u>

③

<u>You too, now.</u>

15쪽으로 넘어가면 드디어 '관용어'의 행진이 이어집니다. 패스트푸드점 등에 가면 주문용 매뉴얼이 있듯이, 점원과 손님이 주고받는 대화는 거의 '관용어'로 구성되어 있어요. 동료에게 지시를 내리던 앞 페이지와는 달리, 여기에서 에드는 노부인을 상대할 때 정중한 접객 용어를 활용하며 대화를 나누고 있죠. 따라서 생략된 단어도 없어요.

노부인의 대화문에서도 에드 못지않게 관용어가 눈에 띕니다. 선배 캐릭터는 특히 관용어를 사용하는 경향이 있어요. 따라서 침착한 성격을 드러내고 싶을 때는 다소 고풍스런 관용어

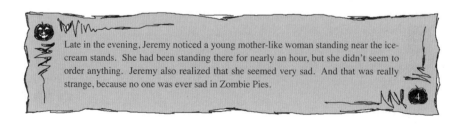

Late in the evening, Jeremy noticed a young mother-like woman standing near the ice-cream stands. She had been standing there for nearly an hour, but she didn't seem to order anything. Jeremy also realized that she seemed very sad. And that was really strange, because no one was ever sad in Zombie Pies.

④

를 사용하면 효과적입니다.

노부인의 관용구 중에서 특히 주목을 끄는 부분은 God bless you와 now, 두 가지입니다.

God bless you(①)를 말 그대로 풀이하면 '신이 당신을 축복하기를'이라는 의미에요. 매우 과장된 표현으로 느껴지지만, 기독교가 일상생활에 녹아들어 있는 미국에서는 Thank you very much와 큰 차이가 없지요.

now(③)는 매우 편리한 단어예요. 원래 '지금'이란 시간을 의미하지만, 이 대화에서처럼 문장의 앞이나 뒤에 놓여서 부록으로 쓰이기도 합니다. 이 경우는 '지금'이 아니라 '자', '그래', '그럼'처럼 별 의미 없이 '간격'을 두는 말로 쓰였어요. 전에 등장했던 You know 등과 비슷하지요. 대화를 한 박자 쉬어가고 싶을 때 등장하는 필수품이랍니다.

에드의 대화문 중 처음 나오는 두 문장과 마지막의 Have a nice day(②)는 계산대 너머로 손님과 대화를 주고받을 때 사용하는 전형적인 표현입니다. 말실수가 용납되지 않는 근무 현장에서는 모든 동작과 질문에 대해 미리 '관용어'로 준비된 표현을 사용하는 것이 일반적이에요. 특히 계산대에서는 손님을 다루는 속도에 따라 매상이 결정되므로 말을 할 때마다 일일이 표현을 고민할 여유가 없습니다. 에드 역시 노부인과 주고받은 표현을 다른 손님에게도 반복해서 사용하겠지요.

사실 관용구의 표현이 늘어날수록 매끄럽고 뛰어난 언변이 됩니다. 마음 편히 회화를 주고받고 싶다면 '관용구'를 많이 익히세요. 적절히 활용하면 말실수를 피할 수도 있으니까요.

단, 관용구는 편한 반면 늘 들어오던 표현이므로 진실한 마음을 상대에게 전하기는 힘들답니다. 사랑 고백이나 사과의 말은 다소 서투르더라도 자신이 직접 고민한 표현을 말할 때 오히려 애정이 느껴져요.

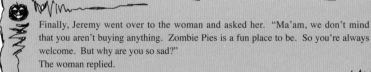

Finally, Jeremy went over to the woman and asked her. "Ma'am, we don't mind that you aren't buying anything. Zombie Pies is a fun place to be. So you're always welcome. But why are you so sad?"
The woman replied.
"My son lives in that hospital across the street."

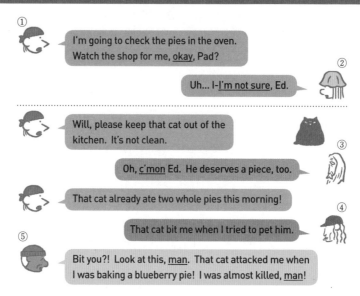

I'm going to check the pies in the oven.
Watch the shop for me, <u>okay</u>, Pad?

Uh... I-I'<u>m not sure</u>, Ed.

Will, please keep that cat out of the kitchen. It's not clean.

Oh, <u>c'mon</u> Ed. He deserves a piece, too.

That cat already ate two whole pies this morning!

That cat bit me when I tried to pet him.

Bit you?! Look at this, <u>man</u>. That cat attacked me when I was baking a blueberry pie! I was almost killed, <u>man</u>!

에드의 okay(①), 패디의 I'm not sure(②) 등도 관용구지만 이 부분에서 가장 눈에 띄는 표현은 역시 윌리의 c'mon(③)입니다. come on을 축약한 표현으로 일반적으로 '이리 오세요'라는 의미로 생각하기 쉽지만, '으음, 괜찮은데 해보지 그래요'와 같은 뉘앙스로 말을 걸 때 사용하기도 해요. 사용 빈도는 오히려 후자가 더 많을 수도 있어요. 자신과 의견이 다른 사람에게 '이쪽 의견으로 오세요'와 같은 의미로 말을 건네는 것입니다.

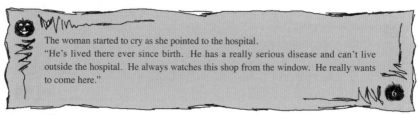

The woman started to cry as she pointed to the hospital.
"He's lived there ever since birth. He has a really serious disease and can't live outside the hospital. He always watches this shop from the window. He really wants to come here."

6

disease = 질병

George, watch out!

Oh-oh... He's gonna kill me now.

⑥

George, RUN!

bite

attack

kill

E-Ed!!

⑦

Sorry, Pad. Be back in a minute!

N-No, Ed!! You need to come back, n-now!

대화의 뒷부분에는 영어만의 독특한 묘미를 느낄 수 있는 요소가 등장합니다. 그 요소란 '단어의 업그레이드'입니다. 비지스가 'bit(물다)당했다'(④)고 푸념하자 조지는 훨씬 더 과장해서 'attack(공격)당했다'(⑤)란 화살표를 사용해서 되받아치죠. 영어는 같은 의미라도 일상적인 표현에서 매우 과장된 표현까지 강도에 따라 단계별로 단어가 준비되어 있습니다. 이를 활용해서 단어들을 적절히 바꾸면 조지가 화살표를 과장된 표현으로 '업그레이드'하듯이 대화를 재치 있게 주고받을 수 있답니다. bite→attack에 뒤이어 화살표가 마지막에는 kill(⑥)이 되었네요. 꽤나 고양이의 공격이 두려웠던 모양이군요.

문장을 보고 곧 눈치 챘겠지만 ⑦에서는 I'll이 생략되었습니다. 원래는 I'll be back in a minute로 이 문장도 자주 사용되는 관용구예요. '1분 이내'라는 의미지만 실제 이미지는 '곧' 정도라고 할 수 있지요. 더 짧게 in a second(1초 이내)라고 표현하기도 해요.

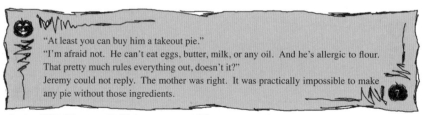

"At least you can buy him a takeout pie."
"I'm afraid not. He can't eat eggs, butter, milk, or any oil. And he's allergic to flour. That pretty much rules everything out, doesn't it?"
Jeremy could not reply. The mother was right. It was practically impossible to make any pie without those ingredients.

⑦

allergic = 알레르기의 rules = 규제하다 practically = 사실상 ingredients = 재료

You wait for me here, <u>okay</u>?

 <u>Sir</u>. You asked me to... Shut the door, <u>you moron</u>.

How is your business?

①

 <u>Great, sir</u>. Zombie Pies is really taking off. <u>You should see the</u> <u>numbers</u>. <u>We're the fastest growing chain</u> in the whole...

Good. Close it down.

 Uh... <u>excuse me</u>?

②

<u>I said</u>, close down the pie shops. I need the space to promote the rehabilitation project.

 ....

③

Did you, or did you not, hear me?

 I... I can't do that, sir. Even if it's your order. It's my shop. The kids love my shops. They really love Zombie Pies. Please let me keep the shops. <u>I really need this</u>.

Your <u>so-called</u> shops will last for maybe another six months. Then they'll get tired of your pies and your shops will be forgotten.

④

 I'll try harder! <u>I'll make it work</u>! Please give me a chance to... ⑤

Quiet.

⑥

Father...

<u>I said</u>, shut up! Billy Bob, turn up the sound.

⑦

"I'm sorry to have bothered you. I'll leave now. But thank you for listening. At least, I'll give him this pamphlet." The mother left with that.

Jeremy was shocked. He couldn't imagine a childhood without any pies. No. Not just pies. No cookies, no chocolate, no ice cream...

8

bothered = 귀찮게 하다 pamphlet = 팸플릿

이 부분에서 제레미 부자가 나누는 대화는 마치 회사의 상사와 신입사원, 군대의 상관과 부하가 주고받는 말투 같지 않나요. 아버지의 대화문은 반론을 일절 용납하지 않는 강경한 어조로, 화살표로 시작하는 명령문을 많이 포함하고 있어요. 이에 비해 제레미의 대화문에는 sir를 붙인 경어체 문장이 많고 마지막에 딱 한 번 '아버지'를 부를 때도(⑥) 흔히 사용하는 Dad를 쓰지 않았어요. 대신 매우 서먹서먹한 태도로 Father란 단어를 사용하고 있네요. 게다가 그 말조차 아버지가 도중에 잘라버렸어요.

You should see the numbers(①, 숫자를 봐주세요), We're the fastest growing chain(①, 단연 눈에 띄게 성장하고 있는 체인점입니다), I really need this(③, 정말 필요합니다), I'll make it work(④, 성공시키겠습니다/it은 '좀비 파이') 등은 모두 어려운 문장처럼 보이지만 이런 상황에서 자주 사용되는 관용구의 하나입니다. 역으로 이런 표현은 대화문에서만 쓰여요.

대화의 중반에서 마지막까지 제레미 아버지가 대화문을 시작할 때 사용한 I said—(②, ⑦)도 관용구입니다. 문장의 첫머리에 두고, 자신이 방금 전에 한 말을 반복하면서 자신의 의견을 상대에게 강요할 때 쓰는 표현이지요.

그리고 제레미 아버지가 말한 마지막 문장(⑦)도 전형적인 관용구입니다. 영어로 '시끄럽다'고 말할 때 대표적인 표현이 바로 shut up이에요. shut은 '철컥 닫다'란 의미로 '입 다물어'라는 의미예요. 그 앞에 나온 Quiet(⑤)은 shut up과 의미는 같지만 더 품위 있는 표현으로 학교에서 선생님 등이 학생들을 조용히 시킬 때 사용한답니다.

제레미 부자가 나누는 대화에는 c'mon처럼 허물없는 사이에서 쓸 수 있는 관용구가 좀처럼 나오지 않아 매우 냉랭한 분위기마저 풍겨요. 제레미는 과연 어떤 기분으로 아버지의 말을 듣고 있었을까요?

That night, Jeremy went home to his laboratory and looked through all his recipes. But it was apparent that pies were impossible to make without at least some sort of oil. Jeremy tried to give up many times, but his mind kept reminding him that there was "a child with no candy" somewhere.

laboratory = 연구실 apparent = 명백한

①
...<u>As you can see</u>, a small miracle has happened here on the deserted northwest side of Everville. People are returning to this <u>once well-known</u> shopping district. A twenty-nine-year-old man, Ed Wishbone, has started a small pie shop in the ruins of an old trailer. This is his kitchen. He says that all of his utensils are fully sanitized and everything is safe and clean. <u>Let's ask Mr. Wishbone himself about his pies</u>.

Do you really make these pies in that backyard? They're really good. Sweet... but not too sweet.

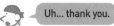

Uh... thank you.

Are you thinking of entering the state pie festival this weekend?

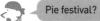

Pie festival?

The Annual State Pie Festival is held this year at the Everville Mall. You should consider entering. The prize this year is twenty thousand dollars!

I... I don't know. I really...

YEAH!!

② I think your customers know.

③
So now <u>you've seen it</u>, one man's journey to save the old streets of Everville. And from the way people are gathering, <u>who knows</u>? He just might succeed. <u>This is Glen Hamperton reporting from Ever...</u>

뉴스 영어는 매우 독특합니다. 기본적으로 문어체에 가깝고 한 문장에 들어 있는 정보량이 너무 많아 처음에는 당황스러울 수도 있어요. 주인공과 조연으로 구성된 한 문장에 설명이 긴 화장문이 붙어 있는 경우가 많기 때문이지요. 몇 행만으로 모든 상황을 설명해야 하는 뉴스에서는 기회만 있으면 문장 곳곳에 정보를 넣습니다. 본문 중에서도 에드가 '29세의 남성'이라는 사실을 설명하고자, Ed Wishbone이란 이름 앞에 무리해서 twenty-nine-year-old man 이란 화장품을 붙여서 설명하고 있지요(①). 하지만 뉴스에 나오는 문장은 이런 정보를 제공하는 문구들을 따로 떼어서 보면 의외로 쉽습니다. 어려워 보여도 사실은 매우 단순해요. 리포터의 첫 대화문도 정보를 끼워 넣은 부분을 삭제하고 보면 아래와 같은 문장이 돼요.

A miracle has happened in Everville. People are coming back to Ghost Avenue. Ed Wishbone has started a pie shop here. This is his kitchen. He says all his utensils are clean. Let's ask Mr. wishbone.

이 내용에 화장품이나 부록의 형태로 될 수 있는 한 구체적인 정보를 많이 첨가해서 드라마틱한 내용으로 꾸미면('this once well-known/한때 유명했던'을 붙이는 등) 리포터의 첫 대화문이 되는 거예요.

문장 ③에는 뉴스 현장에서 중계방송을 하고 있는 스튜디오로 마이크를 넘길 때 으레 하는 관용구가 많이 나옵니다. CNN(Cable News Network)을 보고 있으면 자주 들을 수 있는 표현들이에요. 리포터가 보도 내용을 전하고 자신의 이름을 말하면서 끝맺는 것은 미국 뉴스의 전통적인 방식이거든요. 이때 자주 사용하는 관용구가 who knows예요. 이해하기 어려우면 이 문장을 통째로 삭제하고 읽어도 의미는 통합니다. '누가 (가능성이 없다고) 알 수 있겠는가?'라고 시청자에게 되물음으로써 '어쩌면 가능성이 있을지도 모른다'는 사실을 넌지시 암시하는 방식이지요. 이와 비슷한 관용구로 God only knows(오직 신만이 알고 있다)라는 대중적인 표현도 있지만, 이 경우는 '가능성은 있지만 지금으로선 절망적'이란 뉘앙스를 풍겨요.

참고로 도중에 리포터가 무심코 발언한 I think your customers know(②)는 아주 일상적인 표현이어서 리포터로서가 아니라 한 사람의 인간으로서 발언한 감정적인 코멘트라는 것도 알 수 있어요 .

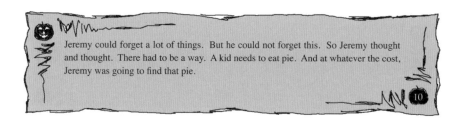

Jeremy could forget a lot of things. But he could not forget this. So Jeremy thought and thought. There had to be a way. A kid needs to eat pie. And at whatever the cost, Jeremy was going to find that pie.

① This is bad. <u>We can't afford</u> having this man become any more popular than he is now.

Yes, sir.

② As for this pie festival... <u>You might as well</u> have that chance of yours. Stop this man from winning the contest and perhaps I will reconsider the termination of your enterprise.

Will... will you really...

③ Do you, or do you not, want a chance?

④ Yes, sir. I'll try my best.

Your best is far from enough. Try harder.

Billy Bob, come here.

 It's okay. I'm used to it. Nothing new.

 Early the next morning, a child named Archie Donnaheim awoke in bed, still holding the pamphlet his mother had brought him. He cried to sleep last night looking at the pamphlet. He knew that he would never go to Zombie Pies. He woke up from bed and looked out of his third-floor window.

제레미 아버지의 대화문(①)에는 살짝 변형된 화살표가 등장합니다. afford는 본래 '~을 살 수 있다'란 의미로 쓰이는 단어예요. 구체적인 예를 들어볼까요. 한 부인이 고가의 제품을 사려다가 선뜻 사지 못하고 가게 입구에서 망설이자 남편이 '사도 괜찮을까?'라고 묻고 부인이 We can afford it이라고 대답하는 상황이에요. 이 영문을 직역하면 '우리는 그 물건을 살 수 있다'라는 뜻이지만, 실제 의미는 '그 제품을 사기 위해서라면 그만큼의 대가(이 문장에서는 '돈')를 지불해도 괜찮다'는 의미이지요. 이 대화문에서는 'afford할 수 없다'고 부정형으로 되어 있으므로, 제레미 아버지는 '에드가 유명해지는 것'을 위해서는 '어떤 대가도 지불할 수 없다'는 뜻이겠죠? 즉 에드가 유명해지는 것을 용납할 수 없다는 의미입니다.

You might as well(②)이란 표현도 일종의 관용구지만 이해하기 어려우면 단순히 You can이나 You may로 바꿔보길 바랍니다. 의미는 같지만 You might as well이 더 근사한 느낌을 주는 동시에 well에는 '타협의 결과 어쩔 수 없이'라는 뉘앙스도 담겨 있어요. 우리말로는 '~하는 편이 낫다'라는 표현과 비슷해요. 상황을 이해하고 받아들인다는 의미 외에 '별 수 없이'라는 의미도 포함하고 있고, 주로 윗사람이 아랫사람에게 말하는 인상을 줍니다.

중반에 또 하나 어려운 표현이 나오네요(③). Do you, or do you not, want a chance?는 본래 Do you want a chance, or do you not want a chance?지만 단도직입적인 느낌을 주기 위해 제레미 아버지가 일부러 최소한의 단어만을 이용해서 표현한 거예요. 내심 안절부절 못하고 있음을 엿볼 수 있는 대화문이지요.

문장 ④에서는 언어유희의 묘미를 살짝 맛볼 수 있습니다. 원래 I'll try my best라는 표현은 겸손하게 의욕을 표출할 때 사용하는 관용구예요. 하지만 여기서는 제레미의 아버지가 이를 겸손함이 아니라 의욕 부족으로 받아들여서 '네가 말하는 최선으로는 부족해'라고 비꼬듯이 대꾸하고 있습니다.

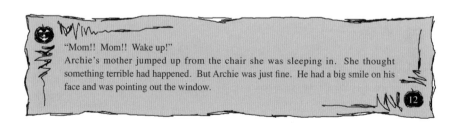

"Mom!! Mom!! Wake up!"
Archie's mother jumped up from the chair she was sleeping in. She thought something terrible had happened. But Archie was just fine. He had a big smile on his face and was pointing out the window.

12

73

Now, *that* is something you don't see everyday.

Damned if I'm seeing that.

Frank's good with animals, that's for sure.

That's not an animal. That's a beast.

조지의 첫 대화문에 나오는 Damned(①)
는 〈빅팻캣과 고스트 애비뉴〉에도 나왔던 표
현으로 강조를 나타내는 단어입니다. '이 멋
진 광경을 실제로 보고 있다'라는 의미로, 조
지의 강한 놀람을 표현했어요. 관용구라서
얼른 의미를 파악하기 어려울 뿐이죠.

Yo, Ed. Apples done, man. What next?

Wow. You're getting faster everyday. Well... maybe you can help Willy and Pad clean the ovens.

이 페이지에서도 '단어의 업그레이드'를
이용해서 에드가 비꼬듯이 말하고 있네요
(②). animal→beast에 나타난 단어의 업

Sure thing.

그레이드는 우리말로 바꿔도 의미가 통합니다. 확실히 에드의 고양이는 '동물'이라기보다는
'짐승'에 가까울 수도 있어요.

조지는 때때로 문장의 끝에 man을 붙이는데(③), 이 man 자체에는 별 의미가 없습니다.
우리말의 '~했다고'와 같이 매우 대중적인 말버릇이지요. 굳이 설명하자면 리듬감을 주기 위
해 넣은 단어입니다.

Sure thing(④)은 Sure와 의미는 거의 비슷하지만 Gotcha와 마찬가지로 '나한테 맡겨'라
는 뉘앙스로 한 말이에요.

Archie's mother couldn't believe her eyes. Outside the window, there was a set just like the inside of Zombie Pies floating in the air. Someone had used a crane to build a giant landscape outside the window. And before she could say anything, the door opened and Zombie Pies music poured in. ⑬

crane = 기중기 landscape = 풍경

pp.32~35 말싸움과 슬랭

 Wishbone.

 I'm afraid we're closed.

① Take it. It's the entry form for this weekend's pie contest.

 Take it, Wishbone! You think you're so good. Come prove it.

I don't want to be in a contest. This shop is all I want. Please leave us alone. ②

③ You lying coward. You would love to win, but you're afraid you'll lose. I bet you've never fought for anything in your whole life.

......

 Wishbone! Stop ignoring me!

Shop! You call this dump a shop!?
A Magic Pie Shop, huh? What does magic mean anyway!? Do you disappear or something?

You need to...

이 부분은 말싸움을 하는 장면입니다. 우리말도 마찬가지지만 영어로 말싸움을 할 때는 관용구가 많이 쓰여요. 화가 치밀어 냉정하게 생각할 수 없으므로 머리에 떠오르는 대로 관용구를 연발하기 일쑤겠죠? 이 장면의 제레미 역시 다르지 않답니다.

 A bunch of zombies marched in and started to dance. It was just like in the stores. Zombies, monsters, smoke, and flame. It was like hell. A hell that was better than any heaven. Archie's mother covered her mouth and was about to cry when Jeremy entered the room.

영어로 말싸움을 할 때 상대의 감정을 건드리기 위해 자주 등장하는 화살표가 prove (①)입니다.

합리주의를 표방하는 미국인다운 사고방식을 엿볼 수 있죠? 어쨌든 '증거를 대라'고 상대를 압박하는 거예요.

bet도 prove처럼 상대의 감정을 건드리기 위해 등장한 화살표입니다(③). I bet은 비아냥거리며 '내기를 해도 좋지만 결과는 틀림없을 것이다'라는 의미로 상대를 약 올리기 위해 쓰여요.

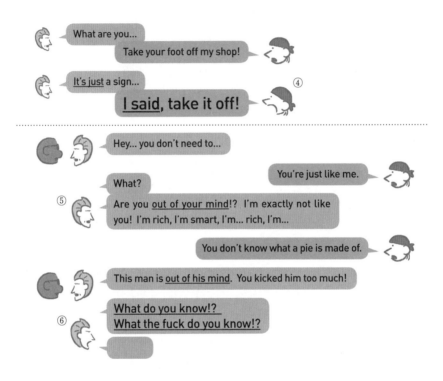

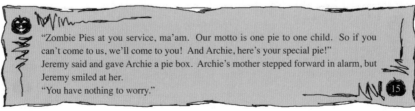

motto = 모토

이에 비해 에드의 leave us (me) alone (②)은 괴롭힘을 당하는 사람이 쓰는 관용구입니다. 실제로 혼자 있고 싶다는 의미가 아니라 '건드리지 말라'는 의미예요. 이런 관용구들은 실제로 초등학교 운동장에서 자주 들을 수 있는 표현들입니다.

또 말싸움을 할 때 자주 쓰이는 관용구로는 단연 슬랭이 대표적이에요. 슬랭이라 불리는 일련의 속어들은 대개 표현이 저속하기 때문에 좀처럼 영어 참고서 등에는 소개되지 않아요. 그 이유는 슬랭이 대부분 천박하거나 폭력적이고 인종차별적인 의미를 지니기 때문이기도 하지만, 우리말로는 슬랭에 해당하는 표현이 없어서 설명이 매우 어렵기 때문이기도 합니다.

미국에 가면 곧 눈치 챌 테지만, 사실 슬랭이 매우 일상적으로 쓰여요. 그럼에도 불구하고 미국 내에서는 학교에서 슬랭을 가르치는 일이 결코 없습니다. 오히려 전면적으로 금지하는 경우가 일반적이죠. 또한 사전에도 거의 실려 있지 않고요.

제레미가 불쑥 내뱉은 fuck (⑥)이란 단어는 슬랭을 대표하는 단어 중의 하나로, 할리우드 액션 영화를 보고 있으면 수차례 들을 수 있습니다. 이미 앞에서 설명해서 잘 알고 있는 damn도 마찬가지에요.

이 fuck이란 단어가 슬랭으로 쓰일 때는 별 의미 없이 문장 어디든 삽입되어 매우 강경한 강조어가 됩니다. 우리말로 옮길 때는 대응하는 단어가 없어서 어쩔 수 없이 '제기랄'이나 '젠장' 등으로 표현되지만 사실 이렇게 옮겨서는 이 단어의 강렬한 효과가 전달되지 않아요.

fuck이란 단어가 초래하는 강렬한 효과는 우리말로는 설명이 불가능해요. 어떻게 해서든 이 단어의 파장을 느껴보고 싶다면 자신이 알고 있는 단어 중 차마 입 밖에 낼 수 없을 만큼 가장 험한 말을 떠올려보세요. 그리고 일반 회화 사이에 불쑥 삽입되어서 마치 문장을 꾸며주는 화장품처럼 쓰인다고 생각해보세요. 이제 조금은 fuck의 쓰임이 짐작이 가나요?

어쨌든 상식 있는 일반인이 이런 단어를 쓸 때는 이미 전후 사정을 생각할 수 없을 만큼 화가 난 상태라는 것만큼은 알아두세요. 자주 들어오던 단어임에도 불구하고 fuck은 분명히 일종의 '금지어'이니까요.

제레미의 아버지가 자주 쓰던 I said라는 표현을 여기에서는 에드가 사용하고 있군요(④).

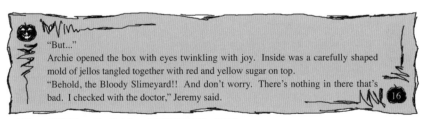

"But..."
Archie opened the box with eyes twinkling with joy. Inside was a carefully shaped mold of jellos tangled together with red and yellow sugar on top.
"Behold, the Bloody Slimeyard!! And don't worry. There's nothing in there that's bad. I checked with the doctor," Jeremy said.

twinkling = 반짝이다 mold = 틀 jellos = 젤로(젤리를 뜻하는 상표명)

소중한 간판이 부서져서 에드도 몹시 화가 치민 상태라는 것을 알 수 있습니다.

I'm exactly not like you(⑤)는 재미있는 문장이에요. 보통은 exactly를 붙이지 않거든요. 우리말로도 '정확히 다르다'라고는 거의 말하지 않는답니다. 하지만 이 부분에서 제레미는 에드가 한 말이 몹시 거슬렸는지 굳이 exactly를 써서 어색한 문장을 만들면서까지 부정하고 있어요. (우리말로 하면 '이 이상 다를 수 없을 만큼 다르다'쯤이 될까요.) 어디든 not을 붙이면 부정이 되어버리는 영어의 편리함을 활용한 대화문입니다. 제레미도 에드의 날카로운 표현에 속으로는 뜨끔했을지도 모르죠.

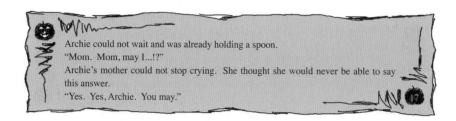

That's enough(①)에서 That이 무엇인지 생각하면 오히려 어려워집니다. 엄밀히 말하면 That은 'BB(Billy Bob)가 한 일(에드에게 폭력을 휘두른 일)'로 이미 enough(충분)하니까 이제 그만하라는 의미지만, 실제로는 That's가 있으나 없으나 상관없어요. Enough!라는 단어가 단독으로 쓰여도 '관용구'가 되기 때문입니다. 싸움을 말리거나 지나친 행동을 저지하려고 할 때 소리를 지르듯이 쓰일 때가 많지만, 이 부분에서는 강조를 하기 위해 제대로 문장의 형식을 갖춰서 쓴 거예요. that은 어떤 단어의 대역으로도 쓰이기 때문에 문장의 형식을 갖추기 위한 주인공으로 가장 손쉽게 쓰인답니다. 바로 이 때문에 That's를 썼을 뿐이에요.

제레미는 문장 ②를 말하고 나서 자리를 떠나는데, 여기서의 see you는 떠날 때 협박하는 느낌을 주기 위해 쓴 말입니다. 이런 협박에 가까운 대화문은 문장의 길이가 짧아야 더 실감이 나요. 그래서 강하지는 않더라도 명령조의 뉘앙스를 풍기기 위해 주인공인 I'll이 문장에서 생략되었어요.

다음에 나오는 조지의 대화문에서는 조지의 개성이 잘 드러납니다. 조지가 말한 첫 대화문인 You all right?(③)은 본래 Are you all right?이에요. 마지막 문장에 나오는 ain't는 제대로 쓰면 isn't이지만 지방에 따라서는 때때로 변형된 형태로 쓰기도 해요. 조지는 사소한 일에는 신경을 쓰지 않는답니다. 대단치 않은 실수는 누구나 저지르는 것이고 문법적으로는 다소 틀린 표현이 오히려 조지의 개성을 드러내는 문장이 된 거죠.

무엇보다 에드가 처음으로 상대에 맞서 대항했으므로 조지가 말한 대로 Cheer up!해야 합니다! 여기서 쓰인 화살표 cheer는 환희에 찬 목소리나 응원하는 목소리를 뜻하니까요. 그 목소리를 up, 즉 높이라고 했으니, 다시 말해 '힘내!'라는 의미로 쓰인 관용구입니다. Yeah!

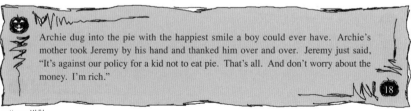

Archie dug into the pie with the happiest smile a boy could ever have. Archie's mother took Jeremy by his hand and thanked him over and over. Jeremy just said, "It's against our policy for a kid not to eat pie. That's all. And don't worry about the money. I'm rich."

18

policy = 방침

Ed! That's mustard.

It's okay. It's my new pie.

Ed. That's mustard.

<u>Of course</u>, it's mustard. It's a mustard pie.

<u>It's not that bad.</u>

<u>Here.</u> I baked one earlier today. <u>Have a taste.</u>

Go ahead. <u>Have a taste.</u>

① Uh, Ed. <u>I'm happy to</u> have the honor of participating in this... this science experiment.

It's not an experiment.

② Oh, I'm sure that my sacrifice will someday be useful to the further development of mankind. <u>Well</u>, <u>so long</u> everybody.

이 장면에서는 Willy가 '단어의 업그레이드'를 통해서 모든 사람의 웃음을 자아냈습니다. 평소라면 I'll try the pie라고 말할 것을 honor, participating, science experiment 등 수상 소감을 말할 때나 등장할 만한 단어를 섞어서 매우 과장된 표현으로 말하고 있어요(①).

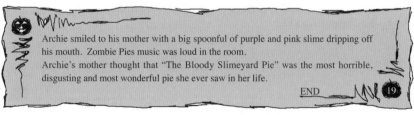

Archie smiled to his mother with a big spoonful of purple and pink slime dripping off his mouth. Zombie Pies music was loud in the room.
Archie's mother thought that "The Bloody Slimeyard Pie" was the most horrible, disgusting and most wonderful pie she ever saw in her life.

END 19

disgusting = 혐오스러운

'단어의 업그레이드'는 지금까지 수차례 등장했지만, 재미있는 회화가 되려면 빠질 수 없는 요소입니다. 영어는 우리말처럼 말투가 다양하지 않아요. 남성의 말투(이런 말투인가?), 여성의 말투(이런 말투일지도 몰라?), 할아버지, 할머니 말투(이런 말투를 말하는구나?) 등 우리말은 연령, 성별, 사회적 배경 등에 따라 특색이 있을 뿐 아니라 '경어'까지 있으므로 대화문에 감정을 반영하기가 쉽지요.

그러나 영어는 어떤 연령이나 성별이든지 대화문 자체에 큰 차이를 반영할 수는 없습니다. 따라서 개성을 드러내기 위해서는 '단어의 선택'이 중요해요. 지금까지 소개한 '관용구' 중에서 어느 것을 내 것으로 할지도 '단어 선택'의 하나에 해당합니다. 그러나 한 걸음 더 나아가 단어의 수준이나 '이 단어가 풍기는 이미지가 나와 맞을까'를 생각해서 택하면 말투에 자신의 개성이 묻어 나옵니다. 특히 배우나 화살표 등은 의미가 같은 단어가 여러 개 있으므로 그 중 어떤 단어를 선택해서 일상적으로 사용하느냐에 따라 그 사람의 이미지가 결정돼요. 예를 들어 '말하다'란 의미에 해당하는 화살표를 생각해보세요.

say / speak / tell / state / suggest / mention / remark / pronounce

정해진 순서는 없지만 일반적으로 단어가 길고 복잡할수록 머리가 좋다거나 과장, 강조, 권위 등의 이미지를 풍깁니다. 그 이유는 길고 복잡한 단어는 일상에서 잘 사용하지 않기 때문이지요. 앞에서도 Ed 일행이 attack, kill 등 일상에서는 그다지 들을 일이 없는 단어를 써서 과장했던 장면이 있었습니다. 이야기의 중반에서는 제레미 아버지가 일부러 어려운 단어를 나열해서 상대를 위압하려는 말투를 쓰기도 했지요. 이 페이지에서도 윌리가 평소라면 I'll try the pie로 그칠 말을 Uh, Ed로 시작하면서 대화문을 점점 과장해서①, ② 좌중을 웃음바다로 만들었습니다.

이처럼 '단어 선택'은 영어에서 빠질 수 없는 중요한 요소입니다. 단, 어떤 단어에 어떤 이미지가 있는지는 사전에 실려 있지 않아요. 이야기를 읽으면서 중간에 나올 때마다 살펴보고 무의식적으로 스스로 이미지를 그려보는 수밖에 없습니다. 바로 이 과정이 영어책을 읽는 즐거움이라고 할 수 있어요!

The smell!? Just with the smell!? <u>No way</u>!!

<u>I'm telling you</u>! It's not that bad!

Hey, Willy. You can get up now. <u>We got your point.</u> Willy?

 No! It's not the pie! It's his heart! It's doing it again!

What?

Prof! <u>C'mon</u>! Prof!

BeeJees! <u>What the hell is going on</u>!?

 <u>Don't worry.</u> It's not your pie.
Willy's heart is in a real bad condition.

Why isn't he in a hospital?

 Because hospitals cost money.

Use mine.

 Hospital costs lots of money. At least two grand a
week. And that's without any treatment.

He's not responding!

Oh no... <u>This is bad, man.</u>
<u>This is really bad.</u>

No way도 대중적인 관용구입니다. no는 상당히 강경한 말투예요. 공포 영화 등에서 괴물에 쫓기는 캐릭터가 죽임을 당하기 직전 외치는 단어가 대개 NOOO!이듯이, 믿을 수 없을 만큼 무서운 광경을 목격했을 때 입에서 자연스럽게 나오는 단어가 no입니다. 그러므로 친구지간에 무언가 거절할 때 no를 쓰면 다소 경직된 느낌을 주지요. 그래서 좀 더 부드럽게 순화한 표현이 사용되는데 그것이 바로 no way입니다. 그 뉘앙스를 가장 잘 살리는 우리말이라면 '무리겠는데' 정도가 되겠지만 부정의 느낌이 조금 강한 편이에요.

반대로 대화문에 no가 단독으로 나오면 매우 강한 부정이라고 생각해야 합니다. 이번 작품에도 몇 번 나왔으므로 찾아서 살펴보고 어떤 상황에서 쓰였는지 확인해보세요.

I'm telling you(①)도 관용구입니다. '말했잖아!'라고 말하면서 좀처럼 알아주지 않는 상대에게 강경한 어조로 확인할 때 주로 써요. I said라고 말하면서 자신이 말한 내용을 반복하는 경우와 비슷하지만, I said가 명령조에 가까운 데 비해서 I'm telling you는 설득하는 느낌이지요. 이 장면에서 에드가 I'm telling you라는 표현을 선택한 이유는 상대가 동료이기 때문입니다.

C'mon이 다시 나왔어요(②). 이 부분에서는 비지스가 의식을 잃은 윌리에게 말을 걸기 위해 쓰였습니다. '이쪽 세상으로 돌아와'란 의미로 쓰인 C'mon이지요. 이후에도 C'mon은 몇 차례 등장해요. 가까이 있는 사람을 부를 때는 물론 의견이 다른 사람, 저 세상으로 가버린 사람 등 어떤 의미에서든 자신과 '떨어져 있는 사람'을 부를 때 쓰는, 매우 편리한 관용구가 바로 C'mon입니다.

hell(③)은 fuck만큼은 아니지만 강조 효과가 상당히 있는 슬랭입니다. 기독교권 나라에서 '지옥'을 의미하는 단어는 우리나라 사람이 생각하는 것보다 훨씬 효과가 큰 단어예요. 단, fuck과는 달리 hell 자체는 금지어가 아니기 때문에 쓰면 안 되는 정도입니다.

Isn't there a phone somewhere? We need an ambulance.

You know there isn't a single working phone on this street. <u>Besides</u>…, no ambulance would come here <u>at this time of night</u>.

 Then <u>what are we supposed to do?</u> <u>He's dying, isn't he?</u>

Pray.

 We have to get him to a hospital.

Don't!

①

Why not!? <u>For heaven's sake!</u>

He wanted to die, Wishbone.
If he's going to die, let him die here.

 <u>That's insane!</u>

Wishbone. You're just making this harder. <u>Let him go.</u>

② <u>C'mon</u> and help me. We have to get him to a hospital.

③

<u>I'm telling you</u>, Wishbone. You're just increasing everyone's pain.

 I know I'm naive. I just don't want to give up.
I've given up too many things already.

④

<u>Damn it</u>, Wishbone. Why can't you understand?
<u>It's too late</u>. We're all too late.

 Ed's easy to learn Cooking Kitchen

TODAY'S RECIPE

<u>Grasshopper Pie</u>

A cold chocolate mint pie!

월리가 쓰러진 긴박한 상황에서 에드와 비지스가 심한 의견 충돌을 겪는 장면입니다. 에드도 비지스도 월리를 위해서 하는 말이지만 각각 성장 과정과 쌓아온 경험이 다르기 때문에 아무리 말해도 서로 다른 결론에 도달하네요.

우리나라에서는 '구급차가 오지 않는 경우'를 결코 생각할 수 없지만, 미국에서는 치안이 열악한 지역은 너무 위험하므로 구급대원이라도 생명의 위협을 느낄 수 있어서 충분히 있을 수 있는 일입니다.

우선 For heaven's sake (①)라는 관용구를 살펴볼까요? 기본적으로는 그 직전에 나온 Why not!?이란 질문에 대한 강조 표현입니다. 자신의 생각을 꼭 강조하고 싶을 때 기독교권 나라에서는 천국이나 지옥을 입에 올려서 강한 인상을 줘요. '하나님 나라의 명예를 걸고 도대체 왜?!'라고 소리 지를 만큼, 에드는 '병원에 데리고 가지 말라'는 비지스의 말에 자신의 귀를 의심하지 않을 수 없었어요.

이야기가 후반으로 접어들면서 지금까지 등장했던 '관용구' 중 몇 개가 다시 등장합니다. C'mon (②), Damn it (④) 등은 정말 자주 등장하는 표현이에요. 주목했으면 하는 부분은 이전에 에드가 사용했던 I'm telling you (③)라는 '관용구'를 비지스가 사용했다는 점입니다. 에드와 비지스는 둘 다 그다지 말싸움을 즐기는 성격이 아니기 때문에 이러한 긴박한 상황에서 선택할 수 있는 단어가 자연스럽게 정해져 있는 거예요. I'm telling you는 '말했잖아'라는 의미로, 따지며 달려드는 말투이기는 해도 어딘지 부드러운 느낌이 있는 표현입니다. Big Fat Cat 시리즈에 등장하는 캐릭터 중에서도 사용할 만한 사람과 사용하지 않을 사람이 확연히 구분되고 있어요.

사용할 만한 사람	미묘한 사람	전혀 사용하지 않을 사람

이 그림에서도 알 수 있듯이 '관용구'란 실로 각각 확실한 이미지를 지니고 있습니다. 관용구의 의미보다는 오히려 이미지가 더 중요하다고 해도 과언이 아니에요.

Ingredients
(for the crust)
1 3/4 cup chocolate cookies
1/3 cup melted butter or margarine
(for the filling)
1/2 cup milk

32 large marshmallows
1 tablespoon cacao liqueur
1 3/4 cup whipped cream
few drops mint essence
a sprinkle of green food color
chocolate spray

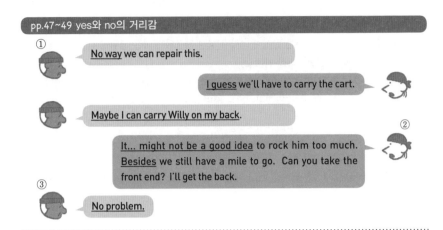

① No way we can repair this.

I guess we'll have to carry the cart.

Maybe I can carry Willy on my back.

It... might not be a good idea to rock him too much. Besides we still have a mile to go. Can you take the front end? I'll get the back. ②

③ No problem.

첫 문장에 No way(①)가 재등장했습니다. 그러나 이 경우는 실제로 '수리할 방법(way)이 없다'는 의미이므로 일반 문장과 가까운 형태예요.

It might not be a good idea(②)는 no의 완곡한 표현 중 하나입니다. 즉 조지의 제안을 부드럽게 거절하고 있어요. 조지의 대화문 중 No problem(③)도 자주 등장하는 관용구 중 하나로 Gotcha나 Sure thing 등과 비슷해요. 즉 yes를 더 강하게 표현한 형태입니다.

Willy?

He's... singing.

Singing? Oh, yeah. I hear it too. ④

마지막의 Oh, yeah(④)는 상당히 거칠게 대꾸한 표현입니다. 평소의 조지라면 No problem 같은 더 부드러운 말투를 썼겠지만, 이 부분에서는 몹시 피곤해서 상대를 배려할 여유가 남아 있지 않았던 모양이네요.

yes와 no는 그 자체만으로는 의외로 별로 쓰이지 않습니다. 이 페이지를 통해서 이 사실을 깨달았을 거예요.

---

1. Heat oven to 180℃. Crush the chocolate cookies into crumbs. Mix crumbs and melted butter. Press mixture firmly against bottom and side of pie plate. Bake about 10 minutes, then cool.

I see trees of green, red roses too
I see them bloom for me and you
And I think to myself
What a wonderful world

I see skies of blue, clouds of white
The bright blessed day and the dark sacred night
And I think to myself
What a wonderful world

I hear babies cry, I watch them grow
They'll learn much more than I'll ever know
And I think to myself
What a wonderful world
Yes I think to myself
What a wonderful world

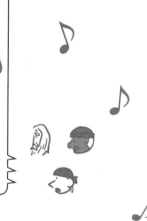

몽롱한 의식 중에 올려다본 밤하늘이 얼마나 아름다운지, 윌리는 자신도 모르게 명곡 〈What a Wonderful World〉(작사·작곡/George David Weiss & Bob Thiele)를 읊조리기 시작합니다. 이 노래를 부른 Louis Armstrong은 세계적으로 알려진 위대한 재즈 뮤지션으로 두터운 입술 때문에 새치모(satchmo=satchel Mouth)라는 애칭으로 불리기도 했지요. Louis Armstrong 말년(1967년도)의 대표작이기도 한 이 노래는 세상의 근원적인 아름다움을 노래한 작품입니다. 우리나라에서도 TV 광고의 배경음악 등으로 종종 쓰였죠. 제목만 들으면 잘 모르더라도 멜로디를 들으면 '아, 이 노래구나' 하는 반길 사람이 많을 거예요. 기회가 있다면 꼭 들어보세요.

2. Heat milk and marshmallows in saucepan over low heat, stirring constantly, until marshmallows are melted. Refrigerate about 20 minutes, stirring occasionally. Gradually stir in cacao liqueur and mint essence.

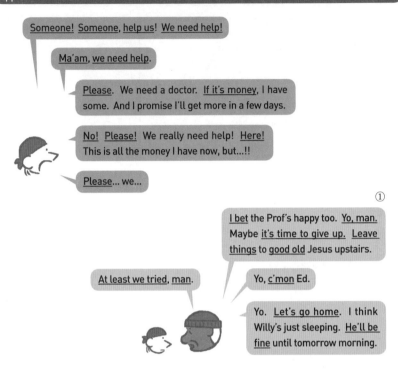

Someone! Someone, help us! We need help!

Ma'am, we need help.

Please. We need a doctor. If it's money, I have some. And I promise I'll get more in a few days.

No! Please! We really need help! Here! This is all the money I have now, but...!!

Please... we...

①

I bet the Prof's happy too. Yo, man. Maybe it's time to give up. Leave things to good old Jesus upstairs.

At least we tried, man.

Yo, c'mon Ed.

Yo. Let's go home. I think Willy's just sleeping. He'll be fine until tomorrow morning.

냉정한 현실을 깨닫게 된 에드는 병원 문 앞에서 털썩 주저앉습니다. 비지스도 과거에 비슷한 경험을 해봤기 때문에 에드를 말렸는지도 몰라요. 에드도 조지도 당황한 탓인지 대화문은 온통 '관용구' 일색이네요. 차분히 생각할 여유가 없어서 머리에 떠오르는 대로 이어서 말하고 있기 때문에 어떻게 보면 당연한 결과겠죠.

3. Beat whipping cream in chilled bowl until stiff. Mix marshmallow mixture into whipped cream. Add food color. Spread in crust. Sprinkle with chocolate. Refrigerate about 4 hours.

이 부분에서 가장 인상적인 대화문은 조지가 말하는 문장(①)입니다. give up하자고 절망에 찬 제안을 하면서도 이어지는 문장에는 어딘지 희망이 묻어 있어요. upstairs(위층, 다시 말해 하늘)에 계신 Jesus(예수=그리스도)에게 뒷일을 맡기자는 표현도 미국에서는 하나의 선택에 포함된답니다. 조지와 에드는 결코 신실한 기독교 신자는 아니지만, 어린 시절부터 기독교에 근거한 교육을 받고 기독교적 가치관이 뿌리내린 사회에서 자랐으므로 급박한 상황에 내몰리자 자연스럽게 이런 표현이 나온 거예요.

제대로 된 가정이라면 일요일엔 교회에 가는 것이 당연하다고 여기는 나라. 그 나라가 바로 미국입니다. 미국의 소설을 읽을 때는 이런 요소를 무시하고 넘어갈 수 없어요. 그러나 미국의 기독교는 우리나라의 종교 이미지와는 상당히 다릅니다. 종교가 도덕의 일부라고 할 만큼 일반적인 사상이니까요. 혹 미국에 여행을 가거든 일요일에 교회에 가보면 미국 문화를 더욱 잘 이해할 수 있을 거예요.

지금까지 다양한 '관용구'를 익혔지만 역시 '관용구' 중에는 기독교와 밀접한 연관이 있는 표현이 많이 있습니다. 기독교의 기본 사상만이라도 알아두면 많은 책과 영화에 숨겨진 수수께끼를 풀 수 있는 힌트도 얻을 수 있을 거예요.

이런 경우에는 이렇게, 저런 경우에는 저렇게 말한다? 바로 '이렇게', '저렇게'에 해당하는 표현이 관용구로, 일상 회화를 주고받을 때 '관용구'는 무의식적으로 사용됩니다. 해설의 첫 부분에도 썼지만 관용구는 일종의 주문(呪文)과도 같아요. 그 주문을 읊으면 기대되는 효과가 어느 정도 정해져 있는 표현들이기 때문이에요.

Pardon me?라고 하면 상대는 지금 말한 내용을 다시 말해주고, Sure thing이라고 하면 상대는 긍정적인 답변을 들었다며 안심합니다.

주문은 그 주문의 효과를 알고 있으면 편리하지만, 효과를 모를 때는 들어봤자 의미를 알 수 없는 단어를 나열한 것에 불과해요. 그리고 모르는 관용구는 여러 번 들어도 의미를 알 수 없는 것이 당연합니다. 왜냐하면 몇 번이나 반복적으로 사용하는 과정에서 의미가 크게 바뀌어 버린 관용구까지 있기 때문이에요. 예를 들어 For heaven's sake!나 God bless you 등이 이에 해당해요.

자주 사용하는 대화문은 암기해놓으면 회화를 주고받을 때 쉽게 활용할 수 있습니다. 또 본인의 생각과는 달리 엉뚱한 이미지를 상대에게 전달할 위험성도 줄어들어요. 그러므로 자신에게 어울리는 '관용구'를 많이 암기하고 있으면 회화를 주고받는 것이 두렵지 않게 됩니다.

그럼 어떻게 '관용구'를 암기해야 할까요. '관용구'를 볼 때마다 전부 목록으로 만들어서 위에서부터 차례대로 암기해봤자 결국에는 별 소용이 없어요. 일단 많은 문장을 읽고 표현을 익혀두면 그 중에서 자연스럽게 자주 사용하는 표현이 자신만의 관용구가 될 거예요. 그 표현이 자신만의 '관용구' 목록으로 등록되어 언젠가는 '나다운' 말투로 주변에 인식되는 것이죠.

이 책에서는 으레 '관용구'가 나올 때마다 밑줄을 그었지만 사실 처음부터 결정된 '관용구'는 없습니다. 관용구를 '결정하는' 주체는 언제나 나 자신이기 때문이에요.

나만의 말투

에드도 제레미도 다들 자신만의 관용구 목록을 가지고 있습니다. 그리고 그 목록에 같은 표현은 하나도 없어요. 예를 들어 누군가를 칭찬할 때도 〈빅팻캣과 매직 파이 숍〉의 등장인물들은 각각 다른 표현을 사용했어요.

Great!   Good job!   Way to go!   Nice.

Not bad.   Well done. / Sufficient.   ......

영어의 관용구는 종류가 다양합니다. 지겨울 정도로 말해왔지만 그런 관용구를 전부 암기할 필요는 없어요. 왜냐하면 대부분의 관용구는 의미를 따로 생각해보지 않아도 전후의 상황과 인물의 성격을 파악하면 무슨 말을 하고 있는지 짐작할 수 있기 때문이에요.

그리고 각 관용구마다 어떤 이미지가 있는지 이치를 따져가면서 암기하는 것은 사실상 불가능합니다. 예를 들어 Gotcha!는 '젊은이나 불량배 등이 사용하는 거친 말투로, 낙천적이고 매사를 깊이 생각하지 않는 타입의 사람이 완벽하게 이해했음을 나타내는 표현'이라고 정리해서 외우려고 해도 좀처럼 외워지지 않아요. Gotcha!를 다른 책에서 보게 되었을 때 '조지가 사용했던 표현'이라고 생각하면 훨씬 편하고 간단하겠죠? 이야기를 통해서 영어를 익히는 최대의 장점이 바로 이거예요.

앞으로는 대화문 중에 이해가 안 가는 표현이 나오면 '어쨌든 관용구니까' 하고 마음을 편히 먹고 장면의 분위기를 통해서 그 의미를 상상해보거나 단어의 뒤에 숨어 있는 의미를 추측해 보면 됩니다. 그렇게 해도 이해가 가지 않을 때는 건너뛰고 읽는 것도 한 방법이에요.

책에 등장하는 인물도 우리와 같은 인간입니다. 그러므로 어떤 장면과 상황에서 느끼는 감정과 사고, 그리고 입 밖으로 내는 표현이 우리와 크게 다르지 않아요. 즉 관용구라고 해도 자신이 같은 상황에 처했을 때 하게 될 말과 의미는 비슷할 거예요. 다만 사람마다 자신이 즐겨 쓰는 말투가 있을 뿐입니다. 대화문은 처음에는 어려워 보이더라도 침착하게 잘 생각해보면 서서히 의미가 보이기 시작해요.

어려운 대화문에 부딪히거든 머리가 아니라 마음으로 생각할 것! 이것이야말로 영어 회화를 익히는 최대의 요령입니다.

BFC EXTRA SPECIAL

ZOMBIE PIES

REGULAR MENU

ZOMBIE
ADULTS HATE US!

THE PIE FROM HELL

This classic evil blood-red cherry pie will grab your heart out!

$22.95

THE ORIGINAL!

"EYE SEE YOU"

Is that eyeball looking at you? Don't be so sure. Eat them all! The greatest cream puffs!

$22.95

COMES WITH "EYE'S CREAM"

MELTING ICEMAN

Light those candles and watch berry-flavored iceman melt over your ice cream pie!

$22.95

GREAT FOR PARTIES!

WITCH'S BREW

This black cheese filled pie is haunted by   Wocka the Witch   and her cat!

$24.95

WOCKA FLIES!!

GHOST IN THE BOX

Open the 9 doors to random selected flavor pies of the month! But beware, one contains the Red Hot Zombie Blood!

$26.95

ALL NEW PIE!

PIES

BUT THEIR KIDS SURE LOVE US!

ALIEN EGG

Inside the purple alien egg, four different fillings await you!

$29.95

CRACK IT AND SEE!

GREEN SLIME BUCKET

Scoop a big dip of mint slime into your cup of crust!

$24.95

COMPLETE WITH DIPPER!

GRAVEYARD DIG

Dig into the graveyard with shovel spoons (included with pies)! Lucky kid finds the gold medal and gets a free slice of pie!

$24.95

#2 BESTSELLER!

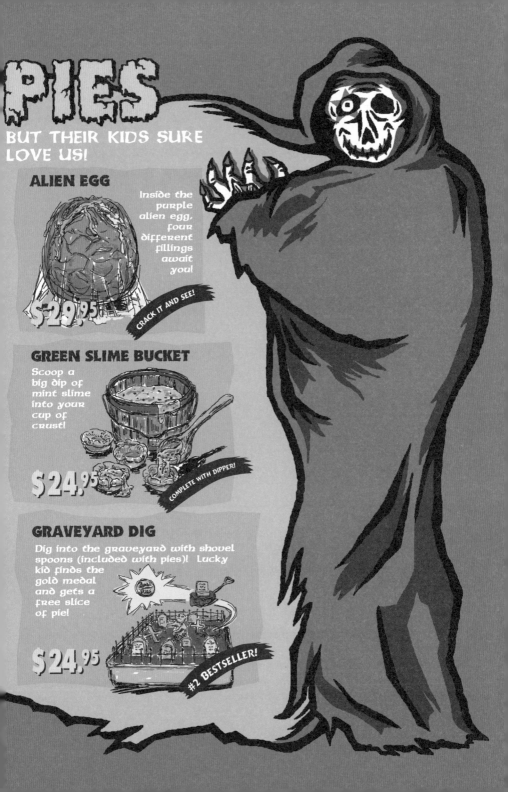

BIG FAT CAT'S
3 COLOR
DICTIONARY

BIG FAT CAT
and the
MAGIC PIE SHOP

빅팻캣의 3색사전
~매직 파이 숍 편~

3색사전 사용법

녹색은 →, ↩ 또는 =   진한 파란색은 두 번째 B′ 상자

빨간색은 A 상자 | 파란색은 B 상자   색깔이 없는 부분은 부록

그래서 이런 문장 형태가 됩니다.

Ed gave the cat a present yesterday.   A→B=B′

일부 이해하기 어려운 문장에는 바로 밑에 짧게나마 자세한 해설을 달아두었습니다.

3색사전은 스토리 부분의 영어 문장을 색깔로 구분하여 문장 형태를 한눈에 알아볼 수 있도록 만든 힌트 북입니다. 물론 '정답'은 아닙니다. 영어 문장을 이해하기 위한 하나의 길잡이로 이용해주세요.

You know this town...   A→B
p.9

첫 네 문장의 you는 바로 독자 여러분입니다. 에버빌에 어서 오세요!

You know this street...   A→B
p.10

And **you know this man.**   A→B
p.12

But **some things have changed** since the last time you saw him.   A↩
p.13

It has been a long month for Ed Wishbone.   A=B

It은 이제 친숙한 '시간'의 대역입니다. 이야기의 서두에 으레 나오는 표현이에요.

"George! Cherry! We need more cherry!" Ed shouted as he handed the last
p.14
slice of cheery pie to a customer.   A→B as A→B

cherry pies에서 pies를 생략했어요.

George was pulling a freshly baked banana chocolate pie out of the barrel
oven.   A=B   barrel oven이 무엇인지는 16쪽의 삽화를 참고하세요.

He shouted to Ed.   A↩

"Gotcha!"   불완전한 문장

George handed the pie over to Paddy and **started running** down the street
to the old cinema.   A→B and (A)→B

They kept several extra pies there, just in case.   A→B

파이가 부족할 case(경우)를 대비해서 extra pies를 영화관에 kept하고 있습니다. just
in case는 관용구로 '만일의 경우를 대비해서'란 뜻이에요.

"W-where do you want this?" Paddy asked Ed.   A→B / B'

　　this는 '패디가 조지에게서 받은 파이'를 말하는 거예요.

p.15

"Below the counter somewhere," Ed told Paddy hurriedly as he turned
back to a waiting customer.   A→B / B' as A↺

"I'm sorry, ma'am.   A=B

　　ma'am은 madam의 줄임형으로 여성에 대한 정중한 호칭입니다. 남성의 경우는 sir이
　　에요.

What can I get for you today?"   A→B

"I'll take a slice of that new lemon pie... and of course, two slices of
blueberry, as usual."   A→B

　　as usual은 '시간'의 부록이에요. 이해하기 어려우면 건너뛰고 읽어도 괜찮아요.

"That'll be 75 cents."   A=B

"Are you sure?   A=B

I feel like I'm cheating you.   A↺

Paying you only 75 cents for such a wonerful pie."   불완전한 문장

"Thank you.   (A)→B

But don't worry.   (A)↺

We're doing fine."   A=B

"Well, God bless you.   A→B

I hope you can do something about this long waiting line though."   A→B

　　do something은 길게 늘어서 있는 줄에 대해서 '뭔가 대책을 세우라'는 뜻이에요.

"I'm sorry, ma'am. I'll try.   A=B   A↺

Have a nice day."   (A)→B

"You too, now."   불완전한 문장

Ed ducked down under the counter for a moment and whispered to Paddy. p.16

A⤵ and (A)⤵   duck은 오리를 일컫지만, 화살표로 쓰일 때는 오리가 머리를 물속으로 쑥 집어넣는 동작을 상상해보세요.

"I'm going to check the pies in the oven.   A=B

Watch the shop for me, okay, Pad?"   (A)→B

"Uh... I-I'm not sure, Ed."   A=B

Paddy looked doubtful but Ed was already dashing out the side door.

A=B but A=B   looked는 seemed로 바꿔도 상관없어요. 어느 쪽이든 A=B의 형태로 이해해보세요.

Behind the trailer, there was a small outdoor kitchen.   A=B

Ed and George had made three ovens out of barrels, steel panels, and pieces of wire.   A→B

The smell of butter and sugar was everywhere.   A=B

Willy and the cat were playing around while Frank watched nearby, sitting in an old toy wagon.   A=B

sitting 이하는 '어떻게'의 부록입니다. toy wagon은 어린이용 장난감으로 바퀴가 달린 작은 탈 것이에요. 보통 뭔가를 태우고 끌고 다니는 놀이기구를 말합니다.

At least, Willy was playing.   A=B

The cat's eyes were much more serious, focused on the pies in the oven.

A=B   serious는 '장난치지 않는 진지한 상태'를 말해요. playing하고 있는 윌리에 비해서 고양이는 훨씬 진지한 태도로 '뭔가'를 주시하고 있어요.

Ed spoke to Willy as he opened the first oven and peeked inside. p.17

A⤵ as A→B and (A)→B

"Will, please keep that cat out of the kitchen.   A→B=B'

고양이를 부엌에서 out한 상태로 유지해달라는 뜻이에요.

It's not clean."   A=B

"Oh, c'mon Ed, He deserves a piece, too," Willy protested.   A→B
> c'mon은 come on의 줄임형으로 다른 사람에게 권유할 때 쓰는 관용구입니다.

"That cat already ate two whole pies this morning!"   A→B

Ed pointed his finger at the cat.   A→B=B'

The cat paid no attention.   A→B

BeeJees grunted.   A↩

He was sitting nearby on an old tractor tire.   A=B

"That cat bit me when I tried to pet him."   A→B

"Bit you?!" George said.   A→B

He had returned from the theater with a cherry pie in his hands.   A↩
> with 이하는 '어떻게'의 부록입니다.

He was still out of breath.   A=B
> 'out of ~'는 무언가가 모조리 밖으로 나와서 '텅 빈' 상태. 이 문장에서는 숨이 끊어질 만
> 큼 놀랐다는 의미입니다.

He showed his free hand to BeeJees.   A→B
> 아무것도 갖고 있지 않은 쪽의 손을 '자유로운 손(free hand)'이라고 표현했어요.

There were four great big slashes on his forearm.   A=B
> 인터넷 주소 등에 사용하는 / 기호를 slash라고 하는데, 실제로 팔뚝에 / 형태로 깊이 파
> 인 흉터가 있었다는 의미입니다.

"Look at this, man.   (A)→B

That cat *attacked* me when I was baking a blueberry pie!   A→B

I was almost killed, man!"   A=B

p.18   "George, watch out!"   A↩
> 문장을 그대로 번역하면 'out(바깥쪽)을 봐'이지만 '조심해'란 의미로 쓰이는 관용구예요.

Ed shouted just in time for George to dodge the cat's jump from behind.

A↺   just in time 이하는 동시에 일어난 일을 나타내는 '시간'의 부록입니다. "dodge ball"이란 게임은 공을 피하는 게임, 즉 피구예요.

The cat soared through the air, a few inches below the cherry pie in George's hand.   A↺
1inch는 2.54cm을 뜻해요. 고양이는 체리 파이의 바로 밑을 통과하는 중입니다.

The cat landed and **turned** back in a very angry motion.   A↺ and (A)↺

George looked at the cat and **gulped.**   A→B and (A)↺

"Oh-oh... **He's gonna kill me** now."   A=B

"George, RUN!" **everybody yelled** together.   A→B

George was already **running,** the cat right behind him in full speed.   A=B

The two dashed through the kitchen and **went** running down Ghost Avenue as **everybody laughed** behind.   A↺ and (A)↺ as A↺
The two는 조지와 고양이에요. as 이하는 동시에 일어난 일을 나타내는 '시간'의 부록입니다.

Ed laughed too, holding a fresh-baked country cheesecake in his hand.   A↺

It had been a long month.   A=B
It은 에드가 고스트 애비뉴에서 생활하기 시작한 때로부터 현재까지를 일컫는 '시간'의 부록입니다.

A long month on Ghost Avenue.   불완전한 문장

It had all begun as a simple joke.   A↺
'그 모든 것은 시작되었다.' 이 문장으로 회상 장면이 시작되어 한동안 이어집니다.

p.19

George, who used to be a handyman, **had made** Ed **a sign** that said "Ed's Magic Pie Shop."   A→B=B'
that 이하는 sign의 화장문입니다.

The sign was a token of appreciation for the pies that Ed baked for the

people in the cinema.   A=B

token of appreciation은 '고마움의 표시'란 의미입니다. 파이 숍의 간판은 에드가 파이를 대접한 데 대한 보답으로 조지가 만든 거예요.

Ed had hung it happily in front of the cinema without much thought.   A→B

But **the other homeless residents of Ghost Avenue who had heard stories about free pie, saw the sign and came** in to get some for themselves.   A=B and (A)↺

who에서 쉼표까지는 화장문으로, 건너뛰고 읽어도 상관없어요. free pie는 free hand와 마찬가지로 '자유롭게 먹을 수 있는 파이', 다시 말해 '무료로 먹을 수 있는 파이'란 의미지요. get some의 뒤에는 pie가 생략되어 있어요.

Some of them even left a few dimes and nickels.   A→B

them은 앞 문장의 'homeless residents'의 대역입니다.

George soon **found an old deserted trailer** at the northern end of Ghost Avenue and **had painted it** with leftover paint.   A→B and (A)→B

The trailer was just the right size to create a small kitchen space, so Ed moved his outdoor kitchen there.   A=B, so A→B

As the days went by, **more and more people started to come buy pies, and not all of them were homeless.**   A→B, and A=B

As에서 쉼표까지는 '시간'의 부록입니다. 뒷부분의 them은 파이를 사러 온 more and more people의 대역이에요.

A few curious passing cars started to stop by, and several kind women who lived nearby had come to buy a slice of pie in the spirit of charity.
A→B, and A↺

They returned for more when they found out the pies were actually good.

A↺   for는 '위해서'란 의미입니다. more의 뒤에 pies가 생략되어 있어요.

p.20 **Now the cat was coming** back down the street.   A=B

Now란 단어를 문두에 써서 회상 장면이 끝났음을 알리고 있어요. Now 이후부터는 현재 장면입니다.

The cat's whiskers were covered with something red.   A=B

　　red는 무엇이 묻은 색일까요? 답은 다음 문장에 있어요.

It pretty much suggested the fate of the cherry pie.   A→B

George came around the corner after the cat, covered with the rest of the
　　cherry pie.   A↺

　　조지의 온몸이 고양이에게 묻어 있던 red로 범벅이었어요.

Ed smiled in spite of losing another pie.   A↺

　　spite는 원래 '악의'를 나타내는 단어이지만 최근에는 좀처럼 단독으로는 쓰이지 않고 관
　　용구인 in spite of(~에도 불구하고) 형태로만 쓰여요.

The others laughed in an uproar.   A↺

　　The others는 other people을 일컫습니다.

They laughed so hard that Ed didn't realize Paddy was shouting.

　　A↺ that A→B　　이해하기 어려우면 that을 지우고 독립된 두 문장으로 생각하면서 읽어
　　보세요.

"E-Ed!!"   불완전한 문장

Ed finally heard Paddy calling him on the third shout and waved a hand at
　　him.   A→B=B' and (A)→B

"Sorry, Pad. Be back in a minute!"   불완전한 문장   (A)=B

"N-NO, Ed!!   불완전한 문장

You need to come back, n-now!"   A→B

Ed's smile faded when he saw that the crowd in front of the shop had
　　grown.   A↺

Grown a lot.   불완전한 문장

　　Grown a lot한 대상은 crowd입니다. 정확히 말하면 The crowd had grown a lot. 즉 '군
　　중이 부쩍 늘었다'예요.

He stood there in awe, his heart beating faster and faster.   A↺

He knew something had gone wrong.   A→B

　　had gone으로 이해가 잘 안 가면 was로 바꿔보세요. 다음의 'He Had ~ child' 문장의
　　had been도 마찬가지입니다.

Jeremy Lightfoot Jr. was afraid of his father.　A=B

He had always been afraid of him, even as a small child.　A=B
　　첫머리의 He는 제레미이고, 뒤이어 나오는 him은 제레미의 아버지입니다.

He felt that his father was always disappointed with him, and therefore,
always angry.　A→B
　　이 문장에서 that 이하는 He(제레미)가 felt한 내용을 나타내요. always angry한 사람
　　은 제레미의 아버지입니다.

He never knew his mother.　A→B

There was nobody to protect him from his father when he was a child.
　　A=B

So he tried desperately to be a good son.　A→B

He tried and tried, but nevertheless his father was always angry.
　　A⤴ and (A)⤴, but A=B

Now, as he stood at the door to his father's study, his hands were shaking.
　　A=B　여기에서도 as가 첫머리에 나왔습니다. 역시 '시간'의 부록이에요.

Jeremy would be thirty-one years old this year, but he still felt like a ten-
year-old boy.　A=B, but A⤴

Jeremy's cat, Mr. Jones, appeared out of nowhere and brushed his tail on
Jeremy's foot.　A⤴ and (A)→B
　　nowhere, 즉 '존재하지 않는 장소'에서 나타났다는 말은 '어디선지 모르게' 갑자기 나타
　　났다는 의미입니다.

Jeremy petted Mr. Jones with a slightly trembling hand.　A→B

It made him feel a little better.　A→B=B'

"You wait for me here, okay?"　A⤴

Mr. Jones purred.　A⤴
　　고양이의 울음소리는 세 단계를 거쳐요. 작고 귀여운 소리부터 차례대로 적어보면 purr
　　→meow →cry입니다.

Jeremy straightened his collar and tie and took a deep breath.
A→B and (A)→B

He grabbed the doorknob and after one last moment of hesitation, turned
it. A→B and (A)→B
after부터 쉼표까지는 '시간'의 부록입니다. doorknob을 grabbed하고 나서 turned하
기까지의 시간을 나타내요.

"Sir. You asked me to…" Jeremy said in a shaking voice as he stepped
inside. A→B as A↺
to 뒤에 하려다가 잘린 말은 come to your office예요.

"Shut the door, you moron." A→B

His father's cold voice filled the room. A→B

Jeremy closed the door and stood nervously beside it. A→B and (A)↺   p.23

His father was watching the morning news on television and didn't even
look back. A=B and (A)↺

The new bodyguard, Billy Bob, was standing at the far wall. A=B

Jeremy didn't know why his father had hired Billy Bob. A→B

He already had two-dozen bodyguards around the house. A→B

But his father had told him Billy Bob was different. A→B / B'

And he was. A=(B)
여기서 he는 Billy Bob입니다. was 뒤에 생략된 단어는 different예요. '다르다'는 의미
를 나타내는 단어 중에서 unique는 긍정적, different는 중립적, weird는 부정적인 의미
가 있어요. 이처럼 단어 선택에 따라 이미지가 조금씩 바뀌어요.

Jeremy had felt it since the first time he had seen the man. A→B

There was a true coldness in the way Billy Bob moved. A=B
the way Billy Bob moved는 'Billy Bob이 움직이는 방식', 다시 말해 'Billy Bob의 동작
입니다'.

And he almost never talked. A↺

p.24

"How is your business?" Jeremy's father asked suddenly.   A→B

Jeremy was surprised.   A=B

His father almost never asked him anything.   A→B / B'

Feeling a sense of relief, Jeremy took a step forward.   A→B
> sense는 '감각'이라는 뜻이에요. 제레미는 안도감을 느끼면서 한 발 앞으로 나왔어요.

"Great, sir. Zombie Pies is really taking off.   불완전한 문장 A=B
> taking off는 '지면에서 take off'했다, 즉 '이륙했다'는 의미입니다. 이 문장에서는 영업
> 이 성황을 이루는 상황을 비행기가 날아오르는 모습에 비유하여 설명했어요.

You should see the numbers.   A→B
> 이 문장에서는 '매상'을 나타낸 숫자입니다.

We're the fastest growing chain in the whole..."   A=B
> 제레미는 in the whole state라고 말하려고 했을까요.

"Good. Close it down."   불완전한 문장   (A)→B
> it은 Zombie Pies의 대역이에요. close down은 '문을 닫다' 다시 말해 '가게를 접다'라
> 는 의미입니다.

Jeremy stopped on his first step, stunned in shock.   A↺

"Uh...excuse me?"   (A)→B

"I said, close down the pie shops.   A→B

I need the space to promote the rehabilitation project."   A→B
> space란 좀비 파이가 없어지고 남은 빈 공간입니다.

Jeremy just stood there, forgetting even to breathe.   A↺

"Did you, or did you not, hear me?" his father demanded, still not moving
   his eyes from the television screen.   A→B
> 첫머리에 나온 Did you 다음에는 hear me를 생략하고, 문장 말미에만 hear me를 썼어
> 요. 본래는 Did you hear me, or did you not hear me?입니다.

"I... I can't do that, sir.   A→B
> that은 Zombie Pies를 close down하는 일입니다.

Even if it's your order.   A=B

It's my shop."   A=B

Jeremy's voice grew smaller and smaller.   A⤴

> grew smaller and smaller를 직역하면 '더 작게 훨씬 더 작게 성장했다'이므로 자칫 모순된 표현처럼 느껴져요. 그러나 grew란 화살표는 '점점 ~해진다'는 의미로도 쓰여요. 이 문장에서는 제레미의 목소리가 점점 작아지는 상황을 상상해보세요.

"The kids love my shops.   A→B

They really love Zombie Pies."   A→B

Jeremy's father said nothing.   A→B

p.25

He was watching the television screen in silence.   A=B

The morning news was showing the top news — something about a government scandal in Washington.   A=B

"Please let me keep the shops.   (A)→B / B'

> let 앞에는 you가 생략되어 있어요. let이란 화살표는 하고자 하는 일을 '허용한다'는 의미가 있어요.

I really need this."   A→B

"Your so-called shops will last for maybe another six months," Jeremy Lightfoot Sr. said finally.   A→B

> another six months는 '앞으로 6개월'입니다. last는 '존속하다'라는 의미로 쓰인 화살표예요.

He spoke in a harsh, cold tone.   A⤴

"Then they'll get tired of your pies and your shops will be forgotten."

> A→B and A=B   they는 손님의 대역입니다. tired는 '피곤하다'는 의미로 자주 쓰이지만 기본적으로 '무언가에 싫증난 상태'를 가리킵니다.

"I'll try harder!   A⤴

I'll make it work!   A→B=B'

> it은 Zombie Pies의 대역입니다.

Please **give me a chance to**..." (A)→B / B'

"Quiet." 불완전한 문장

"Father..." **Jeremy protested.** A→B

"**I said, shut up!**" A→B

Jeremy's father suddenly **raised his voice.** A→B

He leaned forward for a closer look at the television screen. A↺

"**Billy Bob, turn up the sound.**" A→B
> 옛날에는 TV의 채널이나 음량을 조절할 때 TV에 달린 동그란 손잡이를 직접 turn해야
> 했습니다. 지금까지도 당시의 습관이 언어에는 남아 있지요.

Billy Bob took out the remote control and **pushed the volume switch.**
A→B and (A)→B

The voice of a reporter boomed out of the speaker, filling the quiet room
with a sudden burst of excitement. A↺
> filling 이하는 '어떻게'의 부록입니다. quiet room이 with 이하의 소리로 가득했어요.

p.26 "...As you can see, **a small miracle has happened** here on the deserted
northwest side of Everville. A↺

People are returning to this once well-known shopping district. A=B
> this once well-known shopping district는 고스트 애비뉴를 가리켜요.

A twenty-nine-year-old man, Ed Wishbone, has started a small pie shop in
the ruins of an old trailer. A→B

This is his kitchen. A=B

He says that all of his utensils are fully sanitized and everything is safe and
clean. A→B
> 이 문장에서의 that 이하도 He가 say한 내용을 가리킵니다.

Let's ask Mr. Wishbone himself about his pies." (A)→B / B'
> Let's는 Let us를 줄인 것이지만 어려우면 이 문장에서처럼 하나의 화살표로 생각해도

상관없습니다.

The camera moved through the side door of the pie shop and captured a shot of Ed, all red with embarrassment to the rims of his ears.

A↺ and (A)→B   all 이하는 Ed를 꾸며주는 화장품입니다.

Though his father didn't notice, Jeremy opened his eyes wide when he saw Ed on the screen.   A→B

"Do you really make these pies in that backyard?   A→B

you는 Ed의 대역입니다.

They're really good.   A=B

Sweet...but not too sweet."   불완전한 문장

"Uh... thank you."   (A)→B

"Are you thinking of entering the state pie festival this weekend?"   A=B

"Pie festival?"   불완전한 문장

"The Annual State Pie Festival is held this year at the Everville Mall.   A=B

You should consider entering.   A→B

The prize this year is twenty thousand dollars!"   A=B

twenty thousand는 2만입니다.

"I... I don't know. I really..."   A↺   불완전한 문장

Ed was cut off by the loud applause of the customers outside."   A=B

cut off당한 것은 에드의 말이에요.

"I think your customers know."   A→B

에드는 festival에 참가해야 할지 말지 잘 모르겠다고 말했지만 손님들은 어떻게 해야 하는지 잘 알고 있는 듯해요.

The reporter smiled and gave Ed a wink.   A↺ and (A)→B / B'

p.27

"So now you've seen it, one man's journey to save the old streets of
Everville.   A→B
이 문장에서의 you는 TV 시청자의 대역입니다. 에드와 대화하던 리포터가 이번에는 카
메라를 향해 TV 시청자에게 말하고 있어요. it은 쉼표 이하의 내용을 가리키는 대역이에
요. 에드는 본인의 의지와 상관없이 고스트 애비뉴의 구세주로 일컬어지고 말았습니다.

And from the way people are gathering, who knows?   A⊃

He just might succeed.   A⊃

This is Glen Hamperton reporting from Ever..."   A=B
'~가 전해드렸습니다'는 중계를 끝맺을 때 하는 관용구 표현입니다.

p.28

Billy Bob turned the television off.   A→B

Jeremy Senior had raised his hand in the air.   A→B

"This is bad." Jeremy's father said to Billy Bob.   A→B

"We can't afford having this man become any more popular than he is
now."   A→B
he(Ed) is popular now한 상황에서 이보다 more popular한 상황이 될까 봐 제레미의
아버지는 두려워하고 있습니다.

"Yes sir," Billy Bob replied.   A→B

"As for this pie festival..."Jeremy Senior turned his armchair once more
towards his son, took a deep breath, and spoke.   A→B, (A)→B, and (A)⊃

"You might as well have that chance of yours.   A→B

Stop this man from winning the contest and perhaps I will reconsider the
termination of your enterprise."   (A)→B and A→B

"Will... will you really..."   불완전한 문장

"Do you, or do you not, want a chance?"   (A)→B, and A→B
첫머리에 나온 Do you 다음에 생략된 문장은 want a chance입니다.

"Yes, sir. I'll try my best."   불완전한 문장   A→B

"Your best is far from enough. Try harder."   A=B A⤴

That said, Jeremy Senior simply turned away towards Billy Bob.   A⤴

"Billy Bob, come here."   A⤴

p.29

With that, his father seemed to have forgotten he was there.   A=B

He could probably stand there for an hour, but his father would never
    notice him.   A⤴, but A→B

Jeremy Jr. stepped silently out of the room.   A⤴

Only Mr. Jones was waiting for him there, sitting quietly in the middle of the
    long, empty hallway.   A=B

Mr. Jones purred.   A⤴

"It's okay," Jeremy said in a sad voice.   A→B

"I'm used to it. Nothing new."   불완전한 문장   A=B
    it은 제레미 아버지가 취한 행동 전체를 가리키는 대역입니다. 어쨌든 제레미에게는 이런
    상황이 '자주 있었던' 모양이에요.

Jeremy picked the cat up and held it close.   A→B and (A)→B
    close는 화살표로 쓰이기도 하지만 이 문장에서는 부록으로 쓰였고, '가까이'란 의미입
    니다.

Its warmth was comforting in the lifeless coldness of his father's house.
    A=B   Its warmth는 앞 문장에서 제레미가 안아든 고양이의 warmth입니다.

The floor of the corridor was covered with the most expensive carpet on the
    market and the ceiling was decorated with golden ornaments.
    A=B and A=B

Jeremy had lived in this huge mansion for his entire life, but had always felt
    lost in the seemingly endless corridors of the place.   A⤴, but (A)→B
    영어에서 mansion은 대저택 혹은 건물의 한 층을 한 세대가 독차지하는 고급 아파트를
    말합니다. 이처럼 드넓은 공간에 살고 있으므로 뭔가 lost한 느낌이 드는 것도 무리는 아

니겠죠. 단, 제레미는 단순히 넓은 공간 때문이 아니라 인간관계와 같은 고차원적인 의미
에서 felt lost한 느낌이 드는 거죠.

It looked so much like his life. A=B

이 문장에서도 looked를 seemed로 바꿔도 무방합니다.

Fabulous, but empty. 불완전한 문장

---

p.30

"Now, *that* is something you don't see everyday." Ed said to George. A→B

여기서 쓰인 Now도 특별한 의미가 없는 관용구입니다. '날마다 볼 수는 없는 어떤 일'이
무엇인지 답은 앞으로 나오는 '"Damned ~ from Frank's hand.' 문장에 있어요. 아마
Big Fat Cat 사상 처음으로 있는 일일 거예요.

He was staring with widened eyes out of the side door of the Magic Pie Shop. A=B

Geoge poked his head out from behind Ed and saw it too. A→B and (A)→B

"Damned if I'm seeing that," George muttered, nearly dropping the apple he was peeling. A→B

nearly는 almost와 비슷한 의미로 '거의 ~할 뻔했다'입니다.

The cat was eating a piece of piecrust directly from Frank's hand. A=B

If Ed, George, or anybody else tried that, the result would be one less hand.

A=B   that은 앞 문장 전체의 대역이에요.

"Frank's good with animals, that's for sure." George said, shaking his head with disbelief. A→B

Frank's는 Frank is의 줄임형입니다. that's for sure는 관용구로 '확실히'란 의미이지요.

"That's not an animal. That's a beast," Ed said, staring at the cat. A→B

It glared back at him. A⟳

---

p.31

The sunset signaled the end of another day for the Magic Pie Shop. A→B

Newly baked pies were lined on the table, ready for tomorrow.   A=B
line은 '선(線)'이나 '열(列)'을 의미합니다. 이 문장에서는 '줄지어 나열했다'란 뜻이에요.

They gave off the sweet, spicy smell of hot cinnamon.   A→B
They는 앞 문장에 나온 pies의 대역입니다. off는 '멀어져가는 상황'을 나타내요. 파이의
달콤한 냄새가 멀리 공중으로 퍼져나가는 상황을 떠올려보세요.

Hordes of people who had seen the news came rushing in for pies
immediately after the broadcast.   A↺

Ed sold every single slice of pie in the shop before closing for the day.
A→B   '모든 slice를 sold했다'란 표현은 마지막 한 조각까지 다 팔았다는 의미입니다.

"Yo, Ed. Apples done, man. What next?"   불완전한 문장
Apples done은 '사과는 다 했어'라고 가볍게 말을 건네는 느낌이에요.

George tossed the last peeled apple into the water bucket and washed his
hands.   A→B and (A)→B

"Wow. You're getting faster everyday.   A=B
조지가 faster하게 된 것은 조지가 하는 '일'을 말합니다.

Well... maybe you can help Willy and Pad clean the ovens."   A→B=B'

"Sure thing," George said and went out the back door.   A→B and (A)↺

The sun was almost down.   A=B

Orange rays came through the doorway.   A↺

Ed whistled a tune as he knelt down below the counter to get a new bowl.
A→B as A↺

"Wishbone."   불완전한 문장   p.32

Ed froze as he got up.   A↺ as A↺

He found himself face to face with Jeremy Lightfoot Jr.   A→B=B'
face to face는 문자 그대로 얼굴과 얼굴을 맞대고 있는 상태를 말합니다.

He also noticed the big shadow standing behind him.　A→B=B'

"I'm afraid we're closed," Ed replied, almost a whisper.　A→B
　　we're closed는 관용구로 '장사가 끝났다'란 의미입니다.

George and the others were in the backyard kitchen.　A=B

He was alone in the shop.　A=B

Jeremy tossed a flier on top of the counter.　A→B

"Take it.　(A)→B
　　it은 a flier의 대역이에요.

It's the entry form for this weekend's pie contest."　A=B
　　entry는 '참가', form은 '형식'이란 뜻입니다. entry form은 파이 페스티벌 참가를 위해
　　형식상 필요한 서류, 즉 참가 신청서를 말해요.

Ed remained motionless.　A→B

"Take it, Wishbone!" Jeremy said abruptly.　A→B

This made Ed grab the flier.　A→B=B'
　　This는 앞 문장에 나왔던 제레미의 대화문입니다.

"You think you're so good.　A→B

Come prove it."　(A)→B
　　prove는 '증명하다'란 의미로 앞 문장의 내용을 '증명하러 오라'고 말하고 있어요.

p.33

"I don't want to be in a contest," Ed protested to Jeremy.　A→B

"This shop is all I want.　A=B

Please leave us alone."　(A)→B=B'

Jeremy made a face of disgust.　A→B

"You lying coward." he said.　A→B

"You would love to win, but you're afraid you'll lose.　A→B, but A=B

I bet you're never fought for anthing in your whole life."   A→B

you've는 you have의 줄임형입니다.

Ed kept his eyes on Billy Bob.   A→B=B'

But Jeremy's words echoed in his ear.   A↺

Jeremy's words란 한 문장 앞에 나왔던 제레미의 긴 대화문을 말합니다.

"Wishbone! Stop ignoring me!"   불완전한 문장   (A)→B

Jeremy's voice rose even higher in anger.   A↺

He didn't know why he was getting so mad at this man he hardly knew.

A→B   he hardly knew는 this man의 화장문입니다. '잘 알지도 못하는 사람에 불과
한 사람(에드)'에게 제레미는 매우 화가 난 듯하지만······.

He didn't even know why he had come here.   A→B

"Shop! You call this dump a shop!?   불완전한 문장   A→B=B'

A Magic Pie Shop, huh?   불완전한 문장

What does *magic* mean anyway!?   A→B

Do you disappear or something?"   A↺

something은 모든 화살표의 대역으로 쓰일 수 있습니다. '사라지든가, 아니면 뭐라도
하든가?'라고 추궁하고 있네요. 제레미는 앞 문장에서 'magic이라니 대체 무슨 말이
야?!'라고 가게 이름까지 들먹이면서 비아냥거리다가 이런 발언이 나온 거예요.

Jeremy snatched the sign of the Magic Pie Shop.   A→B

He threw it on the ground and stepped on it.   A→B and (A)↺

it은 sign의 대역입니다. stepped는 '밟다'라는 의미로 쓰인 화살표예요.

"You need to..."   A→B

Jeremy never finished his sentence.   A→B

Ed had suddenly grabbed him by the shoulder.   A→B

Jeremy was caught by surprise.   A=B

caught by surprise도 자주 쓰이는 관용구로 surprise에 붙잡혔다는 말은 '(갑작스런
일에) 놀랐다'란 의미입니다.

The man in front of him had suddenly **become angry.**   A=B

The man은 에드를 가리킵니다.

Jeremy noticed this but couldn't understand why.   A→B but (A)→B

this는 '에드가 화난 상태가 된 것'이에요. 제레미는 화가 난 에드에게 신경이 쓰였지만, 왜 화가 났는지는 모르는 듯······.

He kept his foot on the sign.   A→B=B'

"What are you..."   불완전한 문장

"Take your foot off my shop!" Ed said in a surprisingly strong voice.   A→B

에드에게는 간판이 shop 그 자체나 다름없기 때문에 Take your foot off the sign이 아니라 Take your foot off my shop이라고 말하고 있습니다.

"**It's just a sign...**"   A=B

Jeremy was cut off again.   A=B

"**I said, take it off!**"   A→B

p.34

Ed shoved Jeremy off the sign.   A→B=B'

Jeremy lost balance and fell down on his back.   A→B and (A)↺

Billy Bob's large hands grabbed Ed, pulled him over the counter and **threw him** to the ground.   A→B, (A)→B and (A)→B

Ed scrambled over to the sign on the ground and **covered it** with the only thing he had.   (A)↺ and (A)→B

it은 sign의 대역입니다. 에드는 '자신이 갖고 있는 유일한 것'을 희생하더라도 간판을 지키려고 해요. 그 유일한 것이 무엇인지는 다음 문장에 나와요.

His body.   불완전한 문장

Billy Bob was instantly **above him,** kicking him on the side of his chest.   A=B   B상자는 '장소'의 부록으로 생각해도 상관없습니다. him은 에드의 대역이에요.

It hurt badly and Ed couldn't stop coughing.   A↺ and A→B

Dust was flying all around him.   A=B

"Hey... **you don't need to...**"   A→B

Jeremy said to Billy Bob, but **couldn't finish.**   A↺, but (A)↺

He had seen the cold, hard look on Billy Bob's face.   A→B

Billy Bob kicked Ed a second time.   A→B

Ed coughed in pain again, but **refused to get up.**   A↺, but (A)→B
    refused는 '강한 거부'를 나타내는 화살표입니다.

He gritted his teeth together to stop coughing and **looked** straight up at
    Jeremy.   A→B and (A)→B

He tasted blood in his mouth, but **was** no longer scared.   A→B, but (A)=B
    but 이하의 문장은 no longer가 삽입되었으므로 부정문이 됩니다. '이 이상 더는 계속
    되지 않다.' 다시 말해 '더 이상 ~하지 않다'란 뜻이에요.

"You're just like me," **Ed said.**   A→B

p.35

Billy Bob kicked him again.   A→B

"**What?**" **Jeremy cried** out.   A→B

"**Are you out of your mind!?**   A=B
    '제정신이 아니다'란 의미를 'mind(정신)의 바깥'에 있다고 표현했습니다.

I'm exactly **not** like you!   A=B
    여기에서 exactly를 사용한 것은 사실 반칙에 해당합니다.(자세한 설명은 78쪽 참조)

I'm rich, **I'm** smart, **I'm...** rich, **I'm...**"   A=B, A=B, A=B, A=...

"**You don't know what a pie is made of.**"   A→B
    본래 문장은 a pie is made of what입니다. 파이는 무엇으로 만들어질까요?

Jeremy tried hard to laugh but **did not succeed.**   A→B but (A)↺
    한껏 laugh하려고 했지만 succeed하지 못한 모양입니다.

He shouted desperately at Billy Bob.   A↺

"**This man is** out of his mind.   A=B

You kicked him too much!"   A→B

Ed smiled.   A↺
This angered Jeremy even more.   A→B
This는 앞 문장 전체의 대역입니다.

He cried out.   A↺

"What do you know!?   A→B
제레미가 에드에게 '네가 대체 뭘 안다고 그래?!'라고 따지고 있습니다.

What the fuck do you know!?"   A→B

Billy Bob raised his foot over Ed's head.   A→B

Ed squeezed his eyes shut.   A→B

But before Billy Bob could bring his foot down, a flash of red flew through the air.   A↺
before부터 쉼표까지의 문장은 '시간'의 부록이지만 이 문장을 색깔로 구분해보면 Billy Bob could bring his foot down입니다. a flash of red의 정체는 본문 36쪽의 삽화에서 제레미의 얼굴에 떨어진 거예요.

Billy Bob took a step back.   A→B

Jeremy let out a cry of surprise at the same time.   A→B
제레미는 놀라서 입 밖으로(out) 소리를 냈습니다. 즉 놀라서 소리를 질렀다는 의미죠.

"What..."   불완전한 문장

Ed opened his eyes and looked up.   A→B and (A)↺

p.37

Pies were flying through the air!   A=B

Jeremy frantically wiped hot pie from his face, but as he was doing this, some got in his mouth.   A→B, but, A↺
this는 제레미가 얼굴에 묻은 파이를 닦아내는 동작의 대역으로 쓰였습니다. some got in his mouth는 얼굴을 덮친 파이 중 '일부는 입으로 들어갔다'는 의미입니다.

He stopped in silence.   A↺

Several pies hit him but he didn't seem to notice.   A→B but A=B

He just looked straight at Ed.   A→B

Billy Bob had mopped the pie off of his chest and was coming back at Ed.
   A→B and (A)=B

But this time, Jeremy shot his hand out in front of Billy Bob and stopped
   him.   A→B and (A)→B
   him은 Billy Bob의 대역입니다.

"That's enough," Jeremy said to Billy Bob.   A→B

Jeremy and Ed looked at each other one last time.   A→B

The pies had also stopped (probably out of ammunition).   A⤸
   본문 17쪽에 나온 out of breath는 '숨이 차다, 헐떡이다'지만 out of ammunition은 '총
   알이 떨어지다'란 의미입니다.

"See you at the contest," Jeremy said.   A→B

Jeremy straightened his tie and walked off silently.   A→B and (A)⤸

Billy Bob, after a moment of hesitation, followed.   A⤸
   쉼표에서 쉼표까지는 '시간'의 부록입니다. 본래의 문장은 Billy Bob followed (Jeremy)
   이에요.

When Jeremy and Billy Bob were clearly out of sight, George slid down
   from the roof and ran over to Ed.   A⤸ and (A)⤸
   When에서 쉼표까지는 '시간'의 부록입니다. out of sight는 '시야에서 벗어나다'이에요.

p.38

"Ed! Man! You all right?"   불완전한 문장

Ed stood up.   A⤸

In his hands, he held the sign George had painted for him.   A→B
   George 이하는 the sigh의 화장문입니다.

It was broken in half.   A=B

"George... I'm sorry."   A=B

"Hey man, it's just a sign.   A=B
I'll paint you another one tomorrow."   (A)→B / B'
　　one은 sign의 대역입니다.

George laughed as if nothing had happened.   A↺
　　as if 이하는 '아무 일도 일어나지 않았다는 듯'이란 의미입니다.

It was such a light-hearted laugh that Ed smiled a little too.   A=B that A↺
　　이해하기 어려우면 that을 지우고 두 문장으로 이해해도 돼요. light-hearted laugh는
　　'경쾌한 웃음'이란 의미로 매우 기분 좋게 웃는 모습입니다.

"Magic ain't in the sign, man.   A=B
　　ain't는 isn't와 같습니다. 약간 사투리와 같은 말투이지요. '마법이 간판 그 자체에 있지
　　는 않다'는 말은 무슨 말일까요?

Cheer up! We won!"   (A)↺ A↺

With that, Paddy and Willy let out a great big cheer of victory from the roof
　　of the trailer.   A→B
　　that은 방금 전 조지의 대화문 전체를 가리키는 대역입니다.

George patted Ed on the back.   A→B
　　back은 에드의 '뒤' 다시 말해 '등'입니다.

Ed gradually began to laugh out loud too.   A→B

Everyone was laughing except for the cat.   A=B

It just happened to come around the shop at that moment and was
　　confronting the most shocking scene of its life.   A→B and (A)=B
　　it은 고양이의 대역입니다. '해프닝'이라고도 하듯이 happened는 '우연히 일어난 일'을
　　나타내는 화살표예요. 고양이에게 가장 쇼킹한 일이란……

p.39 Midnight.   불완전한 문장

A few hours later, the "ghosts" of Ghost Avenue were safely gathered around the fire inside the cinema.   A=B

Ed had pretty much recovered and was now mixing ingredients for his new
pie.   A↺ and (A)=B

Everybody watched with curiosity as Ed took out a jar of pickles.
A↺ as A→B   pickles는 신맛이 나는 절인 오이로 얇게 썰어서 햄버거의 사이에 끼워
먹어요.

A look of doubt crossed their faces as Ed minced the pickles and threw
them into the bowl.   A→B as A→B and (A)→B

But they managed to remain quiet while Ed added ingredients such as
boiled eggs, grated cheese, and spinach.   A→B
they는 에드 이외의 사람들을 가리키는 대역입니다. such 이하는 ingredients의 구체적
인 내용이에요.

When Ed reached for the small yellow bottle, however, Willy finally spoke
out.   A↺

"Ed! That's mustard," Willy cried as Ed poured mustard from the bottle into
the bowl.   A→B as A→B

Ed heard, but continued to pour the yellow liquid until he had mixed the last
drop into the recipe.   A↺ but (A)→B
에드가 heard한 것은 한 문장 앞의 윌리의 말입니다.

Everybody watched with sour faces.   A↺

Ed looked around the table, saw the faces, and said with a smile, "It's okay.
It's my new pie."   A→B, (A)→B, and (A)→B
faces는 에드 이외의 사람들 얼굴을 말합니다.

"Ed, That's mustard," Willy repeated simply.   A→B

"Of course, it's mustard.   A=B

It's a mustard pie."   A=B

p.40

121

This caused everybody to grimace. A→B=B'
　This는 직전에 나온 에드의 대화문 전체를 가리키는 대역입니다.

"It's not that bad," Ed quickly added. A→B
　that bad란 '모두가 grimace할 만큼' bad하다는 말입니다. 이 문장에서는 그 말을 부정하고 있어요.

Everyone replied with groans and deep sighs. A↺

Ed, a little frustrated, took a freshly baked pie from under the table and placed it in front of everybody. A→B and (A)→B

"Here. I baked one earlier today. 불완전한 문장 A→B
　one은 a mustard pie의 대역입니다.

Have a taste." (A)→B
　taste는 '맛'이란 뜻으로 '한 입맛을 가져봐' 즉 '맛을 보라'는 의미입니다.

Everyone took a step back from the table. A→B

A faint smell of mustard was mixed with the crisp smell of piecrust. A=B

"Go ahead. Have a taste," Ed insisted. A→B

The men looked at each other hopefully, but no one volunteered.
　A→B, but A↺ hopefully는 '반드시 누군가 맛을 봐주리라'는 hope였지만, 머스터드 파이를 맛볼 만큼 배짱이 두둑한 사람은 없었어요.

Reluctantly, they played a game of scissors-paper-stone to deside. A→B

Willy lost. A↺

Willy turned towards the pie with a sad look and found Ed twitching his eyebrows at him. A→B and (A)→B=B'
에드로 하여금 눈썹을 씰룩씰룩 움직이게 한 사람은 윌리입니다.

He smiled quickly. A↺

"Uh, Ed. I'm happy to have the honor of participating in this... this science experiment." 불완전한 문장 A=B

"It's not an experiment," Ed said. A→B

p.41

"Oh, I'm sure that my sacrifice will someday be usedful to the futher development of mankind.   A=B that A=B

useful의 ful은 '가득한 상태'를 나타내는 full에서 온 표현입니다. '가득 찰 때까지 use 할 수 있다' 다시 말해 '도움이 된다'는 뜻이죠.

Well, so long everybody."   불완전한 문장

so long은 '(모두의 행복이) so long하도록'이란 의미가 담긴 관용구로 good-bye란 뜻 입니다.

Willy waved his hand and picked up a piece of the mustard pie.

A→B and (A)→B

He raised it to his nose and smelled it.   A→B and (A)→B

Everyone held their breath.   A→B

'숨을 붙잡다'란 가만히 숨을 죽이고 있는 모습을 나타내요.

After a moment, Willy collapsed to the floor.   A↺

The others burst out laughing.   A→B

조금 전까지 감돌던 긴장감이 풀리고 웃음이 burst out(터져 나오다)했습니다.

"The smell!? Just with the smell!? No way!!" Ed shouted.   A→B

By this time, George, Paddy and Frank were all laughing so hard that they could hardly keep standing.   A=B that A→B

they는 조지, 패디, 프랭크를 가리키는 대역입니다. 그들이 standing한 상태를 지킬 수 없을 만큼 웃음이 터져 나왔습니다.

"I'm telling you! It's not that bad!"   A=B A=B

이 문장에서의 that bad란 '윌리가 넘어질 만큼' bad하다는 의미입니다.

Ed was angry and the others were busy laughing.   A=B and A=B

No one except BeeJees realized that Willy had fallen down awkwardly.

A→B   비지스를 제외하고는 that 이하를 realized한 사람이 없었어요.

BeeJees leaned over the table to whisper to Willy, who was still lying on the floor.   A↺

who 이하는 Willy를 꾸며주는 화장문입니다.

p.42

"Hey, Willy. You can get up now.　불완전한 문장　A⤺

We got your point. Willy?"　불완전한 문장　A→B

　'그 파이 맛이 얼마나 지독한지' 나타내려고 한 point를 '잘 알았다'는 의미입니다.

BeeJees's face turned white when he saw that Willy was lying face down.

　A⤺　　that은 비지스가 본 광경을 가리켜요.

"No! It's not the pie!　불완전한 문장　A=B

　모두가 '파이 때문이겠지'라고 생각하고 있으므로 '그게 아냐!'라고 말하는 비지스이지요.

It's his heart! It's doing it again!"　A=B　A=B

　It's doing it again에서 It은 his heart를 가리키는 대역입니다. 뒤의 it은 확실히는 모르
지만 '심장이 또 그것을 했다'란 뉘앙스예요.

BeeJees jumped across the table to Willy.　A⤺

The others were still laughing.　A=B

"What?" Ed asked.　A→B

He could not hear what BeeJees had said because of the laughter.　A→B

But everyone stopped laughing when BeeJees held up Willy's limp body.

　A→B

"Prof! C'mon! Prof!"　불완전한 문장

　Prof는 Professor의 줄임형입니다. 하지만 평소에는 이렇게 줄여 부르지 않아요.

Ed froze.　A⤺

He couldn't understand what was happening.　A→B

He cried out in almost sheer panic.　A⤺

"BeeJees! What the hell is going on!?"　불완전한 문장　A=B

"Don't worry. It's not your pie," BeeJees turned back and replied quickly.

　A⤺　and　(A)→B

Sweat was running down his forehead.　A=B

"Willy's heart is in a real bad condition."　A=B

All Ed could say was, "Why isn't he in a hospital?"　A=B

"Because hospitals cost money."   A→B

　화살표로서 쓰인 cost는 '(비용이) 든다'는 의미입니다.

"Use mine."   (A)→B

　mine은 my money를 가리켜요.

Ed took his wallet out instantly and held it out to BeeJees.   A→B and (A)→B

A cold felling was rising up in his heart.   A=B

Willy wasn't moving.   A=B

His mouth was half open. as if he had stopped breathing.   A=B

　본문 38쪽에 나왔던 as if가 또 나왔습니다. as if 이하 문장은 현실과 매우 흡사한 가공
　의 이야기를 말해요. '숨이 멎어버린 듯이'란 의미이지요.

Grasping the situation at last, George and Paddy rushed over to Willy and
started slapping his face.   A↺ and (A)→B

The night suddenly seemed a lot darker and colder.   A=B

p.43

"Hospital costs lots of money. At least two grand a week.
And that's without any treatmen," BeeJees said to Ed as he was giving
CPR to Willy.   A→B

　대화문 중에 나온 that은 two grand의 대역입니다. '아무런 치료도 받지 않았는데
　도(입원만 했을 뿐인데) 2천 달러'라고 말하고 있네요. CPR이란 cardiopulmonary
　resuscitation의 약자로 심폐 소생술을 말해요.

"He's not responding!" Paddy cried out, almost in tears.   A→B

"Oh no... This is bad, man. This is really bad."   A=B A=B

George was sweating hard too.   A=B

This was the first time Ed had seen George with a serious face.   A=B

　Ed 이하는 the first time을 꾸며주는 화장문입니다. 조지가 심각한 얼굴을 하고 있던 적
　은 좀처럼 없었다는 의미입니다.

But Ed still couldn't move.   A↺

All he could do was stand there and ask in a dumbfounded voice, "Isn't there a phone somewhere? We need an ambulance."   A=B

"You know there isn't a single working phone on this street." BeeJees said to Ed.   A=B
> 일을 하고 있는 전화, 즉 '사용 가능한 전화'입니다.

He was angry.   A=B
> He는 비지스의 대역입니다.

Probably not angry at Ed, but angry.   불완전한 문장

BeeJees took a deep breath, trying to calm down.   A→B

"Besides..., no ambulance would come here at this time of night."   A↩

"Then what are we supposed to do?   A=B

He's dying, isn't he?"   A=B
> dying은 '지금 죽어 있다'가 아니라 '죽어가고 있다'라는 의미입니다. 완전히 숨이 멎은 상황이라면 He's dead라고 해요.

"Pray," BeeJees answered.   A→B

---

p.44

BeeJees, George, and Paddy were trying to do everything they could.   A=B

But anybody could see this wasn't enough.   A→B
> this는 앞 문장 전체의 대역으로, 할 수 있는 일이 있다면 하려고 했지만 '역부족이었다'라는 의미입니다.

Ed looked desperately around the theater and found a rusty shopping cart by the wall.   A→B and (A)→B

He grabbed the cart and a few old blankets and hurried over to Willy.
> A→B and (A)↩   화살표 뒤에 over가 붙어서 단순히 hurried to Willy했다기보다는 도중에 놓인 물건들을 건너뛰면서 정신없이 달려오는 '기세'를 나타냈어요.

"We have to get him to a hospital."   A→B
> '그를 병원에 데려갈 예정을 가지고 있다', 즉 '병원에 데려가야만 한다'입니다.

Ed reached for Willy's hand but BeeJees slapped his arm away.

    A→B but A→B

"Don't!" 불완전한 문장

"Why not!? For heaven's sake!" 불완전한 문장

"He wanted to die, Wishbone. A→B

If he's going to die, let him die here." (A)→B=B'

    let 앞에 생략된 단어는 you입니다. '그가 여기서 죽는 것을 허용하자', 다시 말해 '그가 여기서 죽을 수 있도록 하자'예요.

"That's insane!" A=B

"Wishbone. You're just making this harder. 불완전한 문장 A=B

    this는 이 상황 전체를 가리키는 대역입니다.

Let him go." (A)→B=B'

    어디로 가게 하는 걸까요. 그곳은 '천국'입니다. 우리말로는 '별세(別世)'와 비슷한 표현이에요.

Ed reached for Willy again. A=B

BeeJees started to stop him, but this time, Ed pushed him away and said to George, "C'mon and help me. We have to get him to a hospital."

    A→B, but, A→B and (A)→B

George nodded and started helping Ed wrap Willy in one of the blankets.

    A↺ and (A)→B

Togerther, they carried Willy over to the shopping cart. A→B

BeeJees just sat there on the ground shaking his head. A↺

"I'm telling you, Wishbone. A=B

You're just increasing everyone's pain." A=B

p.45

Ed finished tucking Willy into the blanket and turned back to BeeJees.
　A→B and (A)↻

He was scared.　A=B

Part of him knew that BeeJees was probably right.　A→B
　him은 에드의 대역으로, '에드의 마음 한구석'이라는 의미입니다.

But another part of him, the warmer, stronger part of him spoke.　A↻
　another part는 앞 문장을 받아서 '에드의 마음 한구석을 제외한 나머지 부분'이에요.

"I know I'm naive.　A→B

I just don't want to give up.　A→B

I've given up too many things already."　A→B

The shopping cart flew through the theater doors, Ed and George pushing it
　from behind.　A↻

BeeJees watched the doors swing from the force of the passing shopping
　cart.　(A)→B=B'

He knew what was going to happen.　A→B
　He는 비지스의 대역으로, '그는 병원에 가면 어떻게 될지 이미 알고 있었다'입니다.

He slumped to the ground, biting his lower lip as the tears came, on by one,
　down his dry cheek.　A↻ as A↻

"Damn it, Wishbone.　(A)→B

Why can't you understand?　A↻

It's too late. We're all too late."　A=B A=B

p.46

The night outside was cold and quiet.　A=B

The moon was almost full, with a perfect sky behind it — no clouds at all.
　A=B

There was no one in sight.　A=B

본문 38쪽의 out of sight와 대구를 이룬 표현으로 이번에는 in sight를 썼네요. '시야가 미치는 범위 내에'라는 뜻이에요. 이 문장에서의 one은 '사람', 그러나 no one이므로 '아무도 없는 상태'가 돼요.

A car passed every once in a while, but other than that, **everything was silent** except for the rattle of their shopping cart.   A↷, but, A=B

once in a while은 '일정 기간 동안 1회' 즉 '가끔'입니다. that은 A car에서 첫 번째 쉼표까지를 가리켜요.

Ed and George pushed the cart down Ghost Avenue until they came to the intersection of Lake Every Drive.   A→B

They crossed the intersection carefully and **continued walking** south.
    A→B and (A)→B   south는 '장소'의 부록으로 '남쪽으로'라는 뜻이에요.

The hospital was about a mile further down the road.   A=B

about은 '대략'이란 의미를 나타내는 접착제입니다. 병원은 이 길을 따라 앞으로 (further) 1마일 정도 되는 지점에 있어요.

It had been easy until then.   A=B

then은 바로 '지금'입니다.

But when they entered the downtown district, **the road changed** uphill.   A↷

It was not a steep incline.   A=B

Perhaps **you wouldn't notice** it if you were walking.   A→B

3색사전 맨 앞에 나온 세 문장과 마찬가지로 you는 독자 여러분을 의미합니다. it은 the road가 uphill로 변화한 것을 가리키는 대역입니다.

But **it made a pretty big difference** if you were a child or a jogger — or even two men pushing a shopping cart.   A→B

The rattle of the rusted cart suddenly **broke** off when one of the front wheels snapped free.   A↷

p.47

The cart was forced to a stop.   A=B

forced는 강한 힘을 의미하는 단어로 'stop할 것을 강요했다'입니다.

Ed knelt down and examined the broken wheel.　A⤴ and (A)→B

George came over to Ed and whispered to him, "No way we can repair this."
　　A⤴ and (A)→B

George was right.　A=B

A sense of unease filled Ed as he said,
"I guess we'll have to carry the cart."　A→B as A→B

"Maybe I can carry Willy on my back," George suggested.　A→B

"It... might not be a good idea to rock him too much.　A=B
　　It은 뒷부분의 to 이하를 가리키는 대역입니다. him은 윌리를 가리켜요. rock은 몸을 격
　　렬하게 뒤흔드는 것을 말해요. 록은 음악의 한 장르이기도 해요.

Besides we still have a mile to go.　A→B
　　to go는 a mile을 꾸며주는 화장문입니다.

Can you take the front end?　A→B
　　front end는 '앞쪽 끝' 다시 말해 '앞쪽 가장자리'입니다.

I'll get the back."　A→B
　　앞 문장의 front와 대구가 되는 표현으로 'back을 들겠다'고 에드가 제안하고 있네요.

"No problem."　불완전한 문장

George nodded.　A⤴

And so they went.　A⤴

Two shadows in the moonlight carrying a man in a shopping cart.
　　불완전한 문장

Sweat rolled down Ed's face, although the first hundred steps were not
　　hard.　A⤴, although A=B
　　first step은 '최초의 한 걸음'으로 hundred가 붙으면 '최초의 백 걸음'이 돼요.

But after ten minutes, the weight of the cart started to feel like the weight
　　of a small car.　A→B
　　카트의 무게가 like 이하와 같이 느껴지기 시작했네요.

Ed's arms and feet were getting weaker and weaker by the moment.　A=B

Ed glanced back over his shoulder.   A↩

He shouldn't have.   A↩

> 보충하면 He shouldn't have glanced back. shouldn't는 '~하지 말았어야 했다'는 뜻입니다.

Fear ran through him as he realized that they still had more than half way to go.   A↩ as (A)→B

> to go를 이해하기 어려우면 건너뛰고 읽어보세요.

The hospital was a small red glow at the top of the hill.   A=B

It wasn't that far, but it seemed miles away.   A=B, but A=B

> It wasn't that far는 앞 문장에서 보았던 만큼 그 정도로 far하지는 않다는 의미입니다.

p.48

The only thing that kept Ed moving was Willy's lifeless face lying within the pile of musty blankets.   A=B

> Ed가 moving하는 상태를 유지시킨 only thing은 B 상자의 핵심 단어입니다.

He had to keep walking.   A→B

He had to.   A→B

*Son. **You are a baker**.*   불완전한 문장   A=B

Professor Willy was the first person who had ever called him a baker.

> A=B   who 이하는 the first person에 붙는 화장문입니다. him은 에드의 대역이에요.

He would never forget that.   A→B

He would never, ever forget that.   A→B

> ever는 never를 한층 더 강조하고 있습니다. never ever는 '절대로 ~하지 않는다'는 뜻의 관용구예요.

One at a time, he took careful steps forward.   A→B

> One at a time은 '하나씩'을 의미하는 관용구입니다.

His legs were weak now.   A=B

One wrong step and he might lose balance.   A→B

and를 사이에 두고 and 왼쪽 상황이 벌어지면 and 오른쪽과 같이 될 것이라는 말이에요.

As they passed the elementary school, Ed thought he heard someone say something in a really soft voice. A→B

B 상자의 문장을 색깔로 구분하면 he heard someone say something in a really soft voice. A→B=B'가 돼요.

He thought that maybe George was saying somthing to encourage himself. A→B

But it wasn't George. A=B

it은 'soft voice의 주인공'을 가리키는 대역입니다.

He could see that, even from behind. A→B

that은 앞 문장 전체의 대역이에요.

Then who — 불완전한 문장

"Willy?" Ed said. A→B

George stopped and looked back. A↺ and (A)↺

Willy's mouth was moving slightly. A=B

Ed leaned forward and listened carefully. A↺ and (A)↺

At first, he thought Willy was just breathing. A→B

But then he was able to hear the soft sounds coming from Willy's mouth. A=B

"He's... singing," Ed said to George with an amazed look. A→B

"Singing?" George gasped and listened. A→B and (A)↺

"Oh, yeah. I hear it too." 불완전한 문장 A→B

It was such a soft and tender voice. A=B

Ed and George started to walk again, but somehow it was easier this time. A→B, but A=B

132

it은 'cart를 메고 walk하는 것'을 가리키는 대역입니다.

The hospital seemed closer and the cart seemed lighter.   A=B and A=B

Ed noticed the full moon in the sky for the first time.   A→B

And in spite of all the chaos, it was still beautiful.   A=B

A comfortable breeze circled around them.   A↺

circle은 '원'을 의미하는 배우지만 여기서는 '원을 그린다'는 의미로 쓰인 화살표입니다.

George began to sing along with Willy.   A→B

along 이하는 '어떻게'에 해당하는 부록입니다.

It was a song Ed had heard millions of times, but he had never realized how beautiful it was until now.   A=B, but A→B

에드에서 쉼표까지는 a song을 꾸며주는 화장문입니다. 뒷부분의 it은 a song의 대역이에요.

Tears formed in his eyes.   A↺

There were so many things he still had to learn.   A=B

he 이하는 so many things를 꾸며주는 화장문으로 '배울 예정을 아직도 가지고 있었다', 즉 '배워야만 한다'는 의미입니다.

The world was so huge and so full of surprises.   A=B

The world is not a mustard pie, Ed.   A=B

No, it wasn't.   (A)=B

it은 The world의 대역입니다. 언뜻 보면 부정문처럼 보이지만 앞 문장의 '세상은 머스터드 파이가 아니야'란 말을 받아서 '(확실히) 그렇지 않았다'라고 말하고 있습니다.

Ed closed his eyes and listened to Willy and George singing.   A→B and (A)→B

And after a moment, he too, joined the song.   A→B

Door.   불완전한 문장

Emergency.   불완전한 문장

p.52

133

Get help.　(A)→B

These were the only thoughts left in Ed's head when they finally reached the emergency entrance of the Everville Hospital.　A=B

These는 바로 앞에 쓰인 세 문장의 대역입니다. 그리고 left in Ed's head는 thoughts (생각)를 꾸며주는 화장문이에요.

He somehow **found some final dregs of stregth** in his legs and **wobbled** up to the doors.　A→B and (A)↺

They were locked.　A=B

Ed banged his fist on the doors.　A→B

"Someone! **Someone, help us!**　불완전한 문장　A→B

We need help!"　A→B

The lights were dark inside.　A=B

Nobody answered Ed's call.　A→B

Ed took a quick look at the shopping cart.　A→B

'에드는 재빠르게 눈길을 한 번 took했다', 다시 말해 '에드는 재빨리 보았다'란 의미죠.

Willy had stopped sining and **was as quiet** as before.　A→B and (A)=B

George was totally **exhausted and was down** on his hands and knees.

A=B and (A)=B　　hands and knees가 땅에 on(접촉)하고 있으므로 땅에 엎드려 있는 모습입니다.

Ed wanted to give up and lie down too, but he continued to hit the door.

A→B, but A→B

Then suddenly, **the sound of a window opening came** from above.　A↺

p.53

Ed backed away a few steps and **found a nurse looking down at them suspiciously.**　A↺ and (A)→B=B'

"Ma'am, we need help," **Ed said.**　A→B

The nurse didn't answer, but her eyes studied Ed and the others carefully
— their dirty ripped clothing, Willy's long beard, and the rusted old
shopping cart.   A↺, but A→B
여기서 studied는 '공부하다'라기보다는 '관찰하다'란 의미로 쓰였어요. nurse가 관찰한
것은 그들의 외모였어요.

"Please. We need a doctor.   불완전한 문장   A→B
If it's money, I have some.   A→B
it은 대역으로 굳이 의미를 따지자면 '당신이 필요로 하는 것'입니다. 그리 하기 쉽지는
않은 말인 '돈이라면 가지고 있다'는 표현을 부드럽게 에둘러 말하고 있네요.

And I promise I'll get more in a few days."   A→B
more의 뒤에 생략된 단어는 money입니다.

The nurse started to close the windows.   A→B

"No! Please! We really need help! Here!" Ed shouted desperately as he
emptied his wallet on the sidewalk.   A→B as A→B
as 이하의 행동과 동시에 에드는 소리를 질렀습니다.

He scattered small change and a few dollar bills around him.   A→B

"This is all the money I have now, but...!!"   A=B

The window closed shut with a cold sound.   A↺
closed와 shut은 둘 다 '문을 닫다'란 의미지만 closed가 일상적으로 문을 닫을 때 쓰는
표현인 데 비해서 shut은 드르륵 소리를 내면서 문을 닫는 느낌이에요. 이 문장에서는
closed가 화살표이므로 shut은 '어떻게'에 해당하는 부록으로 쓰였어요.

Ed was left in the dark with only silence for an answer.   A=B
silence만이 에드에게 answer하고 있었습니다.

"Please... we..."   불완전한 문장

Ed's voice faded as he slumped down on the ground.   A↺ as A↺

George crawled over to Ed and put his hands on Ed's shoulders.   p.54
A↺ and (A)→B

Looking at George's face, Ed realized that George had known this would
happen.　A→B

　　this는 이 상황 전체의 대역입니다. 조지도 이렇게 될 줄 알고 있었나 봐요.

But he had helped him anyway.　A→B

"At least we tried, man."　A↺

George smiled.　A↺

It was a true smile.　A=B

"I bet the Prof's happy too.　A→B

Yo, man. Maybe It's time to give up.　불완전한 문장　A=B

Leave things to good old Jesus upstairs."　(A)→B

Ed sat still on the concrete.　A↺

He knew George was right.　A→B

Just as BeeJees had been right all along.　A=B

　　just as는 '마찬가지로'란 의미입니다. 이 문장은 앞 문장에 붙어서 '어떻게'에 해당하는
　　부록으로도 이해할 수 있어요.

Ed gripped his thighs and lowered his head close to the ground.
　　A→B and (A)→B

He felt hope running out of him.　A→B=B'

　　에드는 hope가 흘러가버리는 것처럼 느꼈어요.

He knew he was about to give up.　A→B

Ed had almost never prayed in his life, but at that moment, he prayed from
the bottom of his heart.　A↺, but, A↺

He prayed for courage.　A→B

The courage not to give up.　불완전한 문장

"Yo, c'mon Ed," George called.　A→B

p.55

As Ed was getting up, something fell out of his chest pocket.　A↺

It floated in the air for a moment, then landed silently on the ground.
　A↺, A↺

Ed picked it up.　A→B

"Yo. Let's go home.　불완전한 문장　(A)↺
I think Willy's just sleeping.　A→B

He'll be fine until tomorrow morning."　A=B

George caught Ed under the arm and helped him to his feet.
　A→B and (A)→B=B'　　him은 에드의 대역입니다. '에드가 발로 지탱하는 것을 도왔
　다' 다시 말해 '에드가 일어서는 것을 도왔다'란 뜻이에요.

Ed was still holding the flier.　A=B

His eyes were glued to the words printed on it.　A=B
　it은 the flier의 대역입니다.

As he read those words,
something Willy had said to him a while before circled around his mind.
　A↺　Willy에서 before까지는 something의 화장문입니다.

Ed. Willy had said.　불완전한 문장　A↺

You are a baker.　A=B

You are a baker.　A=B

You are a baker.　A=B

4권을 끝내며

'매직 파이 숍'에 들러주신 여러분 고맙습니다! 이번 작품부터는 '본문을 이해하기 위한 도움말'인 3색사전의 분량을 대폭 늘렸습니다. 그러니 본문을 읽고 나서 3색사전도 꼭 살펴보시길 바랍니다.

그리고 이번 작품의 해설은 '관용구'에 초점을 맞춰서 썼지만, '관용구'뿐 아니라 모든 단어는 각각의 이미지를 지니고 있습니다.

예를 들어 cold의 뜻은 그냥 '차갑다'가 아닙니다. cold를 듣고 얼음에 손끝이 닿을 때의 감각이 되살아난다면 그 감각이 바로 cold입니다. 이와 달리 cold→'차갑다'→'차가운 감각'과 같은 순서를 거쳐서 의미를 이해하면 이미 영어가 아니라 우리말 감각이 되어버립니다. 우리말이란 필터를 거친 cold인 셈이지요.

하지만 처음에는 이런 과정을 거쳐도 괜찮습니다. 달리 방법이 없기 때문이지요. 처음에는 이렇게 암기를 해보다가 어느 날 인상적인 그림책을 보게 되면, cold라는 단어를 볼 때마다 그림책에서 보았던 눈 내리는 날의 그림이 떠오르게 됩니다. 이렇게 될 때 드디어 그 그림의 이미지가 추상적인 감각으로 마음 한구석에 남아 cold라는 단어를 듣기만 해도 몸이 추워지는 느낌이 들게 되죠.

'단어를 암기한다'는 의미는 바로 이런 것입니다. 'cold＝차갑다'라고 반복해서 되뇌는 것이 아니라 cold라는 단어에 연관되는 추억을 만들어가는 것입니다. '차갑다'란 우리말에 의존하지 않아도 될 만한 추억을.

그림책이 언어 공부에 적절한 이유는 단어에 '추억'을 만들어주기 쉬운 매체이기 때문입니다. 영어에 능통하다는 것은 영어에 대한 추억이 많다는 것입니다. 결코 문법 규칙을 많이 암기하고 있는 것을 의미하지 않습니다.

부디 여러분도 좋은 책을 많이 읽고 좋은 추억을 많이 만들어가길 바랍니다.

그럼 다음에는 파이 페스티벌 현장에서 만나요!

Good luck and happy reading!
Takahiko Mukoyama

이 시리즈는 영문법 교재가 아닙니다. 학습서도 아닙니다. '영어 읽기'를 최우선 목표로 삼고 쓴 책입니다. 몸으로 체험하고 느낄 수 있도록 기존 영문법과는 조금 다른 해석을 실은 부분도 있습니다. 어디까지나 이제 막 영어 읽기를 시작하는 학생들의 이해를 돕기 위해서 의도적으로 도입한 장치들입니다.

STAFF

written and produced by
Takahiko Mukoyama
기획 · 원작 · 글 · 해설
무코야마 다카히코

illustrated by
Tetsuo Takashima
그림 · 캐릭터 디자인
다카시마 데츠오

translated by
Eun Ha Kim
우리말 번역
김은하

art direction by
Yoji Takemura
아트 디렉터
다케무라 요지

technical advice by
Fumika Nagano
테크니컬 어드바이저
나가노 후미카

edited by
Will Books Editorial Department
편집
월북 편집부

English-language editing by
Michael Keezing
영문 교정
마이클 키징

supportive design by
Will Books Design Department
디자인 협력
월북 디자인팀

supervised by
Atsuko Mukoyama
Yoshihiko Mukoyama
감수
무코야마 아츠코(梅光学院大学)
무코야마 요시히코(梅光学院大学)

a studio ET CETERA production
제작
스튜디오 엣세트러

published by
Will Books Publishing Co.
발행
월북

special thanks to:

Mac & Jessie Gorham
Baiko Gakuin University

series dedicated to "Fuwa-chan", our one and only special cat

Studio ET CETERA는 야마구치현 시모노세키시에서 중학교 시절을 함께 보낸 죽마고우들이 의기투합하여 만든 기획 집단입니다. 우리 스튜디오는 작가, 프로듀서, 디자이너, 웹마스터 등 다재다능한 멤버들로 구성되어 있으며 주로 출판 분야에서 엔터테인먼트와 감성이 결합된 작품을 만드는 것을 목표로 하고 있습니다.
ET CETERA라는 이름은 어떤 분류에도 속할 수 있으면서 동시에 어떤 분류에도 온전히 속하지 않는 '그 외'라는 뜻의 et cetera에서 따왔습니다. 우리들만이 할 수 있는 독특한 작품을 만들겠다는 의지의 표현이자 '그 외'에 속하는 많은 사람들을 위해 작품을 만들겠다는 소망이 담긴 이름입니다.

옮긴이 **김은하**

유년 시절을 일본에서 보낸 추억을 잊지 못해 한양대학교에서 일어일문학을 전공했다. 어려서부터 한일 양국의 언어를 익힌 덕분에 번역이 천직이 되었다. 번역하는 틈틈이 바른번역 글밥 아카데미에서 출판 번역 강의를 겸하고 있다. 주요 역서로 〈클래식, 나의 뇌를 깨우다〉, 〈지구 온난화 충격 리포트〉, 〈세계에서 제일 간단한 영어책〉, 〈빅팻캣의 영어 수업: 영어는 안 외우는 것이다〉 등 다수가 있다.

Big Fat Cat and the Magic Pie Shop
빅팻캣과 매직 파이 숍 빅팻캣 시리즈 4

펴낸날 개정판 1쇄 2018년 5월 20일
        개정판 5쇄 2024년 5월 24일
글작가 무코야마 다카히코
그림작가 다카시마 데츠오
옮긴이 김은하

펴낸이 이주애, 홍영완
펴낸곳 (주)윌북
출판등록 제2006-000017호

주소 10881 경기도 파주시 광인사길 217
전자우편 willbooks@naver.com
전화 031-955-3777
팩스 031-955-3778
홈페이지 willbookspub.com
블로그 blog.naver.com/willbooks 포스트 post.naver.com/willbooks
트위터 @onwillbooks 인스타그램 @willbooks_pub

ISBN 979-11-5581-168-9 14740